Copyright Page

Title: HEFE 360: Universal Law and Divine Order

ISBN: 979-8-9987240-4-6

Publisher: HEFE 360 Wealth Ministries

Location: United States (Sovereign 508(c)(1)(A) Jurisdiction)

First Edition

HEFE360
WEALTH MINISTRIES

DISCLAIMER

This book is a sacred teaching tool, spiritual constitution, and doctrinal guide published by **HEFE 360 Wealth Ministries,** a 508(c)(1)(A) faith-based organization operating under First Amendment protection.

The information within this book is provided for **spiritual, educational, and transformational purposes only.** It is not intended as legal advice, financial counsel, tax instruction, or medical diagnosis. While the content includes teachings on trusts, land contracts, legacy planning, energy work, wellness rituals, and international ministry structure, all readers are advised to conduct their own research and, when appropriate, consult with qualified professionals in law, finance, or health.

The authors, publishers, and HEFE 360 Wealth Ministries shall not be held liable for any loss, claim, or action taken based on the use or interpretation of the contents herein. Readers are fully responsible for how they apply this knowledge.

This book is **spiritual doctrine,** not religious dogma or commercial curriculum. All practices, affirmations, rituals, and legacy tools must be approached in alignment with **MAAT** — truth, justice, balance, reciprocity, and divine order.

By reading and engaging with this text, you acknowledge that:

- You are a sovereign being

- You are responsible for your own journey

- You agree to use this information respectfully, spiritually, and lawfully

This is not a product. It is a sacred trust. Use with reverence. **Aṣẹ.**

Table of Contents

HEFE 360: Universal Law and Divine Order

The Sacred Constitution of HEFE 360 Wealth Ministries

Appendices & Sacred Back Matter

HEFE 360: Universal Law and Divine Order

LAW 1 – The Vision of HEFE 360 Wealth Ministries

"To forget who you are is to forget what you were sent to restore."

HEFE 360 Wealth Ministries was born from a sacred realization: that modern spiritual systems have been stripped of their original power, and our people — melanin-rich, lineage-rich, and divinely designed — have been made to forget the laws that once governed heaven, Earth, and self.

This Ministry does not merely teach — it reawakens. It does not convert — it **confirms** what has always been inscribed in your DNA, in your blood, and in the stars above your head.

At the center of our mission is a simple but divine truth:

Wealth is not money. Wealth is alignment.

It is legacy, law, and light. It is structure, sovereignty, and sacred memory restored. It is knowing your bloodline. Reclaiming your spiritual citizenship. Walking in universal law. Activating your divine assignment. And protecting your purpose with the same force that created pyramids, galaxies, and entire civilizations.

What is HEFE 360?

HEFE means: Highest Elevation For Eternity.

360 symbolizes: wholeness, circle, return, and divine completion.

Together, it represents a **complete return to divine law, ancestral knowledge, and spiritual power.**

6

This Ministry is not a religion — it is a **system of divine order**. It is the restoration of ancient spiritual infrastructure. It is a bridge between the old world and the new mission. It is the spiritual arm of a global movement — one that teaches how to live in alignment with the universe while mastering this world's systems for the next generation's freedom.

Why This Book Exists

This is your spiritual textbook. Your manual for sacred alignment. Your roadmap to legacy.

You will learn:

- The 7 Principles of *MAAT* that guided ancient civilization

- The *Universal Laws* that govern all matter, mind, and meaning

- The *42 Declarations of Divine Order* that shaped morality long before Moses

- How to trace your **bloodline** and reclaim **ancestral citizenship**

- How to activate **diplomatic status** lawfully through divine work

- Why your **body, food, and melanin** are sacred technologies

- Why **astrology** is not superstition, but spiritual navigation

- How to turn your house into a **consulate**, your mission into **protection**, and your life into a **legacy** that cannot be erased

Our Ministry is Built on Law, Not Lore

Modern religious institutions often preach belief over knowledge. Faith without understanding. Emotion without order. But the original spiritual systems — the ones practiced by your ancestors in Kemet, Nubia, and Ethiopia — were grounded in law, math, time, nature, and universal alignment.

This Ministry restores that truth.

We teach that **spirit is law**, not fantasy. **Faith is science**, not superstition. And **healing is structure**, not chaos.

The ancient temples of Kemet were not churches — they were **schools, laboratories, and universities.** Every pillar, every symbol, every rite was designed to align the initiate with divine order. That is our goal at HEFE 360: to help you remember what your ancestors lived by instinct — to bring back divine systems that were replaced by false hierarchies.

Reclaiming Our Sacred Inheritance

Our Ministry operates from the understanding that we are not beginning something new — we are **resurrecting something ancient.** Our ancestors left behind blueprints: pyramids that align with stars, temples that encode sacred geometry, scrolls that describe the laws of vibration, balance, and reciprocity. These were not myths — they were manuals for divine living.

We reclaim our **spiritual inheritance** through knowledge of:

- **The laws that governed the Nile Valley civilizations**

- **The real moral systems before colonization**

- **The science of the cosmos, the Earth, and the body as one system**

- **Legacy tools like trusts, titles, and temples** used to protect wealth and wisdom

The names were changed. The books were hidden. The symbols were demonized. But the truth never disappeared — it simply waited for those willing to remember.

Why Wealth Is Sacred

In this ministry, we don't chase money — we **activate wealth.** Wealth is not paper. It is **principle**. It is the ability to **create, control, and protect** your resources — physically, spiritually, and generationally. That is why we teach:

How to own nothing but control everything

How to use law to protect your assets

How to use spirituality to govern your mind

And how to use universal alignment to create heaven on Earth

Our vision is to raise a generation of people who are **financially sovereign, spiritually aligned, and globally recognized** as dignitaries of divine law.

This is not a movement of emotion. It is a movement of **precision**.

A Call to the Chosen

You are not reading this book by accident. You were **called** to remember. You were chosen to reawaken what was buried beneath 400 years of lies, laws, and losses.

This book will not save you — but it will **show you how to realign**, rebuild, and reclaim. The rest is in your hands. Your choices. Your movement. Your discipline.

Welcome to the circle.

Welcome to the order.

Welcome to HEFE 360 Wealth Ministries.

LAW 2 – The 7 Principles of MAAT

Part 1: TRUTH (Ma'at as Divine Reality)

"There is no higher law than Truth." – Kemetic Proverb

In Kemet, Ma'at wasn't just a word — she was a divine force, a goddess, and a standard. **Truth** (Ma'at) was not merely about honesty. It meant **alignment with divine reality**. To speak the truth was to speak in rhythm with the universe.

Ma'at was the **opposite of isfet** — which meant chaos, illusion, falsehood, and imbalance. Speaking or living in falsehood wasn't just wrong — it was spiritually toxic. In ancient times, truth was not subjective. It was cosmic. Measurable. Sacred.

Truth in Practice (Then & Now):

In ancient Kemet:

- Leaders were judged by how they upheld truth in **court, temples, trade, and personal life**

- Scribes recorded only what aligned with observable law and nature

- Initiates of the temples were taught to **speak, write, and live** in truth or be spiritually expelled

Today:

- Living in truth means:
    - Being in **alignment** with who you are
    - Rejecting false identities, colonized religion, and manipulated history
    - Speaking your truth even when it costs comfort

o   Living by **divine law,** not just man-made rules

If you live out of alignment with truth, you attract chaos. You will see confusion in your finances, relationships, health, and mental peace. But when you stand in truth, all of creation recognizes you.

How to Apply TRUTH Today:

- Learn your **true identity and bloodline**

- Study the laws of nature — not just scripture

- Check your **intentions before you speak**

- Don't repeat things that aren't verified — falsehood is spiritual poison

- Build a life rooted in facts, legacy, structure, and law — not fantasy or convenience

Spiritual Affirmation:

"I walk in the truth of my divine origin. I speak only what aligns with creation. I am an embodiment of Ma'at."

Part 2: JUSTICE (Divine Balance and Fairness)

"Without justice, Ma'at cannot stand. And without Ma'at, the world collapses."

In ancient Kemet, **justice was not punishment — it was balance**. The word we now call "justice" meant restoring right order. It meant **rebalancing the scales** when something or someone fell out of alignment. And it began at the personal level — not just in courts, but in the heart, in the home, and in the leadership of the land.

Ma'at as justice taught that the true judge is not man — it is **divine balance**. The ancients did not need police or prisons. They had **principles**. When violations occurred, it wasn't about revenge or power — it was about restoring equilibrium between individuals, families, the land, and the ancestors.

Justice in Practice (Then & Now):

In ancient Kemet:

- Pharaohs were not "kings" — *they were guardians of Ma'at*

- Disputes were settled in **spiritual courts,** with priests, scribes, and elders

- Every citizen was expected to live in a way that **did no harm** to others, the land, or the gods

Today:

- Justice is corrupted by money, race, and power

- We live in a system where imbalance is called "law"

- **Spiritual justice** reminds us that true justice comes from restoring what's right, not just what's legal

To live in justice means:

- You treat others with **fairness, truth, and compassion**

- You hold **yourself accountable** before judging anyone else

- You seek to correct imbalance, not just to win or punish

- You speak up when you see injustice — even when it's unpopular

How to Apply JUSTICE Today:

- In business: Be fair, honest, and transparent — **don't exploit others**

- In relationships: Don't demand what you don't give

- In leadership: Rule with **equity**, not ego

- In society: Understand that systems without Ma'at create destruction

- In spirituality: If you benefit from Ma'at, you must protect Ma'at in the world around you

Justice in Relationships: Sacred Bonds, Sacred Balance

In Ma'at, relationships were not casual — they were **cosmic assignments**. The bond between mother and child, husband and wife, brother and sister, father and son — these were not just social roles. They were **divine connections,** forged by the Creator for the purpose of growth, healing, and generational strength.

To dishonor a relationship was to dishonor **the law of balance itself**. A marriage was not about control — it was about **harmony**. A child was not the property of the parent — they were **a soul to be guided in truth.** True justice in relationships comes not from who is "right" or "wrong," but from **what restores the balance, what honors the Creator,** and **what serves the next generation.**

What This Means Today:

- Don't weaponize emotions to dominate divine unions

- Don't punish your partner or child to feel powerful — seek balance, not control

- Understand that in every dispute, Ma'at is watching:

  o Are your actions restoring harmony?

  o Are your words aligned with truth and healing?

  o Are you honoring your **sacred roles?**

Justice in your home reflects justice in your spirit. If your house is out of order, Ma'at is not present.

Spiritual Affirmation:

"I am a vessel of divine justice. I move in fairness, speak in equity, and restore what has been broken."

Part 3: HARMONY (Spiritual Rhythm and Social Order)

"Harmony is not silence — it is the sacred sound of everything in its rightful place."

Harmony is the invisible thread that holds the universe together. In the teachings of Ma'at, **harmony is the rhythm of divine order.** It's the reason stars don't collide, rivers don't rise past their boundaries, and a baby grows in the womb for nine perfect months.

In ancient Kemet, harmony was both **cosmic and cultural.** It governed the **relationship between heaven and earth,** between kings and the people, between man and his own mind. Where there was disharmony, there was sickness. War. Famine. Mental confusion. So to restore harmony was to restore life.

Harmony in Practice (Then & Now):

In ancient Kemet:

- Architecture was designed with **harmonic ratios** to reflect the divine

- Music and rituals followed **celestial rhythms** (planetary, lunar, solar)

- Society had roles, rites of passage, and sacred rituals to preserve inner and outer peace

Today:

- We live in a world of noise, chaos, overconsumption, and overstimulation

- People are disconnected from nature, from rhythm, from rest

- **Spiritual disharmony shows up as anxiety, depression, addiction, and dis-ease**

But harmony can be restored.

It starts with you.

How to Apply HARMONY Today:

- **Wake and sleep with the sun** — your body is designed for rhythm

- **Speak less, listen more** — harmony requires spiritual hearing

- Clean your home, your temple, your body — **clutter is chaos**

- Respect timing — not every action is for now

- In relationships: Don't dominate. Don't disappear. Flow.

- **Unplug from digital distraction** — Ma'at cannot live in mental noise

- Fast. Breathe. Journal. Touch water. Touch earth. Reconnect.

Harmony doesn't mean there's no conflict — it means there's a higher rhythm guiding you through it. And when you align with that rhythm, the **universe moves in your favor.**

Spiritual Affirmation:

"I am in rhythm with the universe. My thoughts, my breath, my speech, and my actions sing the song of Ma'at."

Part 4: BALANCE (The Sacred Scale Within and Without)

"The scale is sacred — not because it weighs others, but because it weighs you."

Balance is the heart of Ma'at. In every temple of Kemet, the image of Ma'at holding a scale was central. That scale wasn't just about measuring others — it was about measuring **your soul.** In the Hall of Judgment, it is said that your heart was weighed against the **feather of Ma'at**. If your heart was heavy — with lies, ego, greed, or hate — you could not pass into eternal peace.

Balance is not perfection. It is **intentional alignment.** It is the ability to center yourself when the world pushes and pulls. It is the spiritual maturity to not go too far in one direction — whether that's fear or pride, indulgence or self-denial.

Balance in Practice (Then & Now):

In ancient Kemet:

- Leaders were taught to rule with balance — not emotion, not dictatorship

- Sacred rituals and seasonal festivals helped maintain harmony between the people and nature

- Even agriculture followed Ma'at — over-farming or over-consuming was seen as an **offense to the land**

Today:

- People live in extremes: overworking, overthinking, overeating, overreacting

- Balance is seen as boring, but in truth it's the **gateway to peace, clarity, and prosperity**

Without balance, power turns to corruption. Freedom turns to chaos. Spirituality turns into fantasy. And relationships turn into war.

How to Apply BALANCE Today:

- Don't over-give or over-receive — relationships should be **mutual**

- Keep your spiritual practices **balanced** — don't get lost in the metaphysical without applying the physical

- - Balance your schedule: work, rest, reflect, create

- Balance your mind: between logic and intuition, emotion and discipline

- Balance your heart: between love and boundaries

- Don't suppress your pain — but don't let it lead your life either

- Learn the art of **pause** — the power of stillness is where alignment returns

Spiritual Affirmation:

"I walk in balance. I honor both the shadow and the light. I hold myself accountable on the scale of Ma'at."

Part 5: ORDER (Universal Structure & Divine Timing)

"There is a time and place for all things. Ma'at is that time. Ma'at is that place."

Order is the spiritual blueprint behind **all creation**. It is the reason why the sun rises and sets without fail, why the stars form constellations, and why a seed planted in darkness knows how to reach for the light. In Kemet, Ma'at as Order was not about control — it was about **natural design, purpose, and cosmic intelligence.**

Divine order teaches that everything has its **season, cycle, and sequence.** To live outside of order is to **resist your assignment**, to fight the current of the universe. And when you force what is not timed, you create imbalance — spiritually, financially, mentally, and emotionally.

Order in Practice (Then & Now):

In ancient Kemet:

- Temples were built with astronomical precision to align with celestial events

- Society was organized by **function, duty, and divine rhythm** — not classism or competition

- Children were taught **ritual and responsibility**, not just obedience

- **Seasons, moons, and stars** were used to plan everything — from agriculture to spiritual rites

Today:

- We rush. We force. We multitask. We confuse speed with success

- We suffer because we **move out of timing** — wanting blessings we are not prepared to carry

18

- We reject structure and call it "freedom," but true freedom comes from **knowing your rightful place and season**

How to Apply ORDER Today:

- Respect divine timing — if it's not aligned, **don't force it**

- Set routines: your body, mind, and spirit **thrive on rhythm**

- Finish what you start — unfinished tasks create energetic disorder

- Clean your space — external clutter mirrors internal confusion

- Don't envy others' season — focus on mastering your own

- Trust the process — **you are being built as you build**

Divine order doesn't mean your life will be perfect — it means your life will be **in sync**. When you align with the structure of the Creator, you unlock the flow of the Creator.

Spiritual Affirmation:

"I move in divine order. I release chaos and embrace timing. Everything I need is already aligned for me."

Part 6: RECIPROCITY (What You Give Is What You Receive)

"Give, and it shall return — not always from the same hand, but from the same law."

Reciprocity is the engine of the universe. In the teachings of Ma'at, it is known that **every action carries a return**, and every gift carries a responsibility. Reciprocity is not karma — it is **cosmic accounting.** It is the law that governs **exchange, energy, respect, and reward.**

To give without expectation and to receive with humility are both sacred acts. The ancestors understood this deeply. That is why temples had offerings, land had harvest rituals, and people honored each other's time, gifts, and presence. To **violate reciprocity** was to invite imbalance, blockages, and loss.

Reciprocity in Practice (Then & Now):

In ancient Kemet:

- Offerings were left at altars not to bribe the gods, but to maintain **spiritual balance**

- Kings gave land, food, and protection — and the people gave loyalty, labor, and respect

- Elders gave wisdom — and the youth gave honor

- Every gift was met with gratitude and a return, whether physical, energetic, or spiritual

Today:

- People expect much but give little

- Some give too much and wonder why they're drained

- The world is addicted to **taking without restoring** — and that creates spiritual debt

How to Apply RECIPROCITY Today:

- If you take energy, give energy — don't leave people empty

- If someone gives you wisdom, **share the fruit,** not just the praise

- If you're blessed with resources, circulate them with intention

- Don't take advantage of kindness — it has a **spiritual price**

- Don't give to manipulate — give because you are whole

- Know your worth — and only exchange with those who **honor the balance**

Ma'at teaches that what you give returns — **but not always from the same source.** The law may use another door, another time, another form. Trust the law. Protect the exchange.

Spiritual Affirmation:

"I give with intention. I receive with grace. I honor the law of exchange, and all that flows from me returns multiplied."

Part 7: RIGHTEOUSNESS (Uprightness in Spirit, Deed, and Mind)

"The righteous are not perfect — they are aligned."

Righteousness is not **about religion** — it's about alignment. In the teachings of Ma'at, righteousness means to **walk upright** — to be centered, honest, fair, and clean in both your intentions and your actions. It is a spiritual posture — not for show, but for truth.

In Kemet, righteousness wasn't proven by how loud you prayed or how many offerings you gave. It was measured by how you **treated people**, how you **governed yourself**, how you **honored the laws of the universe**, and how you **lived when no one was watching.**

Righteousness was both **internal compass** and **external expression** — a daily practice of integrity, humility, and divine accountability.

Righteousness in Practice (Then & Now):

In ancient Kemet:

- The righteous were those who upheld Ma'at in **all things**, even at personal cost

- Judges, priests, and scribes were selected based on their commitment to Ma'at — not wealth or bloodline

- To be called "Ma'at kheru" — true of voice — meant you lived in righteousness and would be welcomed into eternity

Today:

- Many confuse righteousness with being perfect, religious, or judgmental

- But righteousness is about **living in alignment with truth**, walking in integrity, and doing what is right — even when it's not easy

- It is not about **being above others**, but about **being consistent with your highest self**

How to Apply RIGHTEOUSNESS Today:

- Speak the truth — even when it costs you

- Don't exploit people, platforms, or power

- Return what you borrow. Apologize when you're wrong. Do what you said you would do

- Align your **private self** with your **public self** — don't wear a mask

- Treat every decision as sacred — your life is your temple

- Pray. Fast. Reflect. Realign — not for image, but for truth

Righteousness isn't loud. It's steady. It's clean. It's powerful. And it is the **foundation of spiritual respect** — from your ancestors, from the universe, and from your own soul.

Spiritual Affirmation:

"I live in righteousness. I choose integrity over ego. My life is an offering of truth, and my legacy will testify that I walked in Ma'at."

LAW 3 – Universal Laws That Govern All

"When you master the laws, you stop living by luck."

The universe is not random. It is governed by a divine system of **laws**, just like the Earth is governed by gravity, motion, and magnetism. The ancients knew this — and so they lived not just by rules, but by **principles** written into the structure of creation itself. These are the **Universal Laws.**

While Ma'at gave us the **ethical foundation**, the Universal Laws reveal the **energetic mechanics** of life. They teach us **why things manifest, why we attract certain experiences**, and **how to consciously align** with the divine flow of existence.

When you violate these laws, you suffer. Not because of punishment — but because of **misalignment**. When you master them, life moves differently. You begin to **create intentionally,** not react emotionally.

The 7 Primary Universal Laws We Will Explore:

1. **The Law of Mentalism** – *All is mind. The universe is mental.*

2. **The Law of Correspondence** – *As above, so below. As within, so without.*

3. **The Law of Vibration** – *Everything moves. Nothing rests.*

4. **The Law of Polarity** – *Everything has its opposite — duality is divine.*

5. **The Law of Rhythm** – *Everything flows in cycles — nothing stays the same.*

6. **The Law of Cause and Effect** – *Nothing happens by chance. All action has a return.*

7. **The Law of Gender** – *Everything contains masculine and feminine energy.*

Let's begin with Law 1: **The Law of Mentalism.**

Law 1: The Law of Mentalism – All is Mind

"The universe is mental — held in the mind of the Creator."

Everything begins with thought. Every structure, every war, every movement, every invention — **first existed in the unseen realm of mind.** The Law of Mentalism teaches us that **spirit is mind, and mind is the first substance of creation.**

This means: your reality is a reflection of your dominant thoughts. **Your inner world creates your outer world.** If your mind is filled with fear, lack, and trauma — you will manifest more of it. If it is filled with truth, order, and vision — you will attract alignment

Mentalism in Ancient Kemet:

- The gods were not "beings" but **forces of consciousness**

- Thought (Tehuti) was the first god — representing **divine intelligence**

- Temples were designed to **reprogram the mind,** not just worship

- Initiates were trained to master their mind before anything else — to speak, think, and imagine in alignment with divine law

How to Apply Mentalism Today:

- Guard your thoughts — they are seeds

- Speak with intention — your words shape energy

- Meditate daily — reconnect your mind to source

- Visualize your life with clarity — stop hoping and start programming

- Detox from media, gossip, and mental pollution

- Use affirmations and sacred language to **retrain your subconscious**

- Know that prayer, prophecy, and purpose all begin in **thought first**

Your mind is your first altar. If your thoughts are dirty, your temple is compromised.

Spiritual Affirmation:

"I am the creator of my reality. My thoughts align with divine order. I think with power, purpose, and precision."

LAW 2 – THE LAW OF CORRESPONDENCE

"As above, so below. As within, so without."

This law is a mirror.

It teaches that all planes of existence — the **spiritual, mental, emotional, physical, and cosmic** — are connected by reflection and pattern. What you see in one layer of life, you will see echoed in another. This is how our ancestors decoded the stars, read their bodies, interpreted dreams, and predicted the rise and fall of nations.

Correspondence reveals that the universe is not chaos — it is order repeated at different levels.

Your body mirrors the Earth. Your thoughts mirror your life. Your home mirrors your mind. The macrocosm reflects the microcosm — and vice versa.

Correspondence in Ancient Kemet:

- Temples were built to reflect **heavenly constellations** and cosmic geometry

- The **pyramids mirror Orion's Belt,** reflecting celestial truth on Earth

- The body was understood as a temple, with each organ and energy center aligned to universal principles

- What was seen in the stars was expected to manifest in the Earth and in man

What This Means Spiritually:

If you are in turmoil on the **inside**, don't be surprised when it shows up in your **finances**, your relationships, or your health. If you are in order spiritually and emotionally, you begin to experience peace in the physical world. This is not superstition — it is science. It is law.

When you align your inner world, your outer world begins to obey.

How to Apply the Law of Correspondence Today:

- **Clean your space** — cluttered home = cluttered thoughts

- **Watch your language** — speech reflects your inner programming

- **Pay attention to recurring issues** — the outside is mirroring something you haven't healed within

- Use astrology, journaling, and reflection to track patterns between mind, body, and events

- Realign before reacting — when things go wrong, first look within

The world will always mirror your dominant frequency. Change the root, and the fruit will follow.

Spiritual Affirmation:

"I am the bridge between the seen and the unseen. My inner peace becomes my outer prosperity. I align within, and all things align around me."

LAW 3 – THE LAW OF VIBRATION

"Nothing rests. Everything moves. Everything vibrates."

At the core of all matter, all energy, and all spirit — there is **motion**. The Law of Vibration teaches that everything in the universe is in a constant state of movement. What appears still to the eye is actually **alive with frequency.**

From the cells in your body to the galaxies overhead, from your thoughts to your emotions — **everything carries a vibration**. And that vibration **attracts, repels, or transforms** everything around it.

Vibration in Ancient Kemet:

- The ancients knew the **spoken word was power** — vibration carried intention, magic, and creation

- Temples were built to **amplify resonance** — certain chambers echoed sacred frequencies

- **Sound healing**, drums, chants, and tones were used to align the spirit and heal the body

- High priests and priestesses were trained to **vibrate at higher mental and emotional frequencies** — this gave them spiritual authority

The Power of Frequency in Your Life:

Your **thoughts vibrate**. Your **voice vibrates**. Your **spirit vibrates**.

And all of it sends out a signal that tells the universe what to bring into your life.

- When you vibrate with **fear**, you attract instability.

- When you vibrate with **love**, you attract healing.

- When you vibrate with **gratitude**, doors open.

- When you vibrate with **envy**, blessings delay.

This law teaches you to take control of your vibration — not by faking emotions, but by aligning your spirit with truth, healing, and growth.

How to Apply the Law of Vibration Today:

- Monitor your **mood** — it's your frequency meter

- Use music, chanting, or mantras to shift your energy

- Cut off conversations and environments that bring your frequency down

- Drink clean water, eat electric foods — **they affect your vibration**

- Speak with life, not death — your tongue is a tuning fork

- Journal your emotions daily — releasing low energy makes room for higher frequency

Remember: you don't attract what you want — you attract what you vibrate. Become the frequency of what you desire, and it will find you.

Spiritual Affirmation:

"I am energy in motion. My vibration is sacred. I tune my life to the frequency of truth, peace, and divine creation."

LAW 4 – THE LAW OF POLARITY

"Everything is dual. Everything has poles. Everything has its opposite."

This law reveals that **duality is a divine design,** not a mistake. Every truth has an opposite truth. Every light has a shadow. Every winter has a summer. Every joy has a sorrow. Life is built on **pairs,** and polarity is not here to divide — it exists to **teach, balance, and refine.**

The Law of Polarity teaches us that **contrast is necessary for understanding.** Without darkness, we would not appreciate light. Without failure, we would not understand success. Without pain, we would not value healing.

Polarity in Ancient Kemet:

- The gods were paired as **masculine and feminine, light and dark, creation and destruction**

- Ma'at and Isfet were seen not as "good and evil," but as **order and disorder** — two necessary forces

- Every initiate was taught to master both sides of self — not to suppress the shadow, but to balance it

- Temples contained **symbolic pairs** — two columns, two sphinxes, two doors — to reflect the sacred duality of the universe

What This Law Reveals Spiritually:

Polarity means that nothing is all good or all bad — everything contains **the seed of its opposite.** Your worst failures hold the wisdom for your greatest elevation. Your deepest wounds may unlock your highest calling. This law teaches us to **embrace contrast**, not fight it.

When you understand polarity, **you stop reacting to life emotionally,** and start engaging it spiritually. You see every loss as an opening. Every delay as preparation. Every enemy as a teacher.

How to Apply the Law of Polarity Today:

- Stop running from hard times — ask what they're here to teach

- When someone triggers you, explore the **opposite energy** they're activatin ong

- Journal both your pain and your blessings — they are often connected

- Balance your masculine and feminine energy — assertiveness and intuition, action and reflection

- Don't chase highs — stability comes from **integrating both sides**

You are both shadow and light. The goal is not to destroy one side, but to **master the space between them.**

Spiritual Affirmation:

"I embrace the sacred duality of life. I grow from contrast. I rise from challenge. I walk in balance between all things."

LAW 5 – THE LAW OF RHYTHM

"Everything flows in and out. Everything rises and falls. Rhythm compensates."

Just like the ocean has tides, the moon has phases, and the body has a heartbeat — **everything in creation moves in a rhythm**. The Law of Rhythm teaches us that life unfolds in **cycles**: birth and death, inhale and exhale, abundance and stillness, expansion and retreat.

There are **seasons for everything,** and when you resist these divine rhythms, you suffer. When you align with them, you flow.

This law is not here to scare you with "ups and downs" — it is here to teach you how to **move with divine timing,** rather than fight against it.

Rhythm in Ancient Kemet:

- The Nile was the **heartbeat of Kemet** — it flooded and receded in perfect cycles

- Agricultural, spiritual, and social calendars followed **lunar and solar rhythms**

- Temples held ceremonies based on **equinoxes, solstices, and star movements**

- Fasting, prayer, and offerings were done in cycles to align the people with the divine pulse

Spiritual Meaning of Rhythm:

Everything you experience has a rhythm:

- Joy and grief

- Action and rest

- Gaining and letting go

- Speaking and listening

If you try to **force productivity in a resting season,** or **rush healing in a winter cycle,** you'll burn out, block your growth, and fall into spiritual anxiety. But if you **study your seasons,** honor your body, and trust the process, **you will always be in divine flow.**

How to Apply the Law of Rhythm Today:

- Identify your **personal energetic seasons** — when are you most creative, most inward, most reflective?

- Rest when it's time to rest — don't glorify burnout

- Don't panic when life slows down — it's preparing you for your next rise

- Use the moon cycles (new moon = planting, full moon = releasing)

- Honor your emotions — they come in waves. Ride them, don't drown in them

- Sync with nature — walk, fast, stretch, reflect with the sun and moon

The most successful people, spiritually and materially, **move with rhythm**, not impulse. Rhythm is **divine intelligence in motion.**

Spiritual Affirmation:

"I move in rhythm with the universe. I do not fear the fall or chase the rise. I trust the divine wave that carries me to my highest self."

LAW 6 – THE LAW OF CAUSE AND EFFECT

"Every cause has its effect. Every effect has its cause."

This law is also known as **divine justice** in motion. It governs accountability, **manifestation**, and **spiritual consequence**. Nothing happens by chance. Every thought, word, action, or intention you send out becomes a **cause**, and that cause will **return to you** as an effect — whether you see it immediately or years later.

The Law of Cause and Effect reminds you that **you are never a victim of the universe — you are always in relationship with it.**

Cause and Effect in Ancient Kemet:

Ma'at herself was often represented as this law in action — **weighing the heart** against the feather was the ultimate judgment of causes and consequences

Scribes recorded **deeds and intentions,** not just actions, as part of a person's karmic record

Priests and elders taught initiates that **even thoughts carry weight** and create ripples

Rituals were performed to **cleanse the spiritual body of past causes that still lingered**

Spiritual Truth Behind This Law:

This law is not "punishment" — it is **feedback**. It helps you grow. If you're experiencing lack, look at where you've planted seeds of scarcity. If you are surrounded by confusion, ask where you've spoken or tolerated distortion. And if you are receiving blessings, recognize where you've sown obedience, gratitude, or trust.

- You may not be able to control every outcome — but you can control what you send out.

- How to Apply the Law of Cause and Effect Today:

- Stop asking "Why me?" and start asking "Where did I plant this?"

- Choose your words and actions with **intention** — they echo in eternity

- Reflect on cycles — what patterns keep repeating in your life?

- Heal the root, not just the result

- Sow what you wish to receive — **love, peace, clarity,**

abundance, truth

- Understand that thoughts are also causes — **clean your mind, cleanse your life**

The moment you begin to move intentionally, the **law moves with you** — not against you. Cause wisely. Receive divinely.

Spiritual Affirmation:

"I am the author of my cause. I send out only what I wish to return. I walk with awareness and receive the blessings of alignment."

LAW 7 – THE LAW OF GENDER

"Gender is in everything. Everything has masculine and feminine principles."

This law is not about biology — it is about **energy**. The Law of Gender teaches that **masculine and feminine energies exist within all things** — and both are necessary for creation, growth, balance, and divine purpose.

Masculine energy is **assertive**, logical, structured, and projective.

Feminine energy is **receptive**, intuitive, nurturing, and magnetic.

Every being, regardless of physical gender, contains both. And every process in the universe — from **birth to healing, leadership to love, action to manifestation** — requires both forces working together in harmony.

Gender in Ancient Kemet:

- Kemet revered both **feminine and masculine deities** — Isis (Auset) and Osiris (Asar), Nut and Geb, Sekhmet and Ptah

- Temples trained priests **and** priestesses equally — because wisdom flows through both energies

- Divine creation myths described the universe as birthed through the **union of masculine force and feminine space**

- Every ritual, structure, and spiritual system was designed to honor **both poles** — not dominate one over the other

Spiritual Truth of Gender:

The masculine creates direction. The feminine receives vision. The masculine acts. The feminine attracts. Without the masculine, there is no motion. Without the feminine, there is no meaning.

This law teaches that when your **masculine and feminine energies are out of balance,** you will experience dysfunction:

- Over-masculine: domination, burnout, emotional suppression

- Over-feminine: passivity, emotional overload, indecision

Healing and elevation require both.

How to Apply the Law of Gender Today:

- Develop your **intuition** (feminine) and your **discipline** (masculine)

- In relationships, seek **energy balance** — not just roles or titles

- Don't shame your feminine softness or your masculine strength

- Practice **receiving** as much as you practice **doing**

- Create space for both **logic and emotion, structure and surrender**

- Honor women not as helpers — but as portals of life and wisdom

- Honor men not as rulers — but as guardians of balance and spiritual execution

- You are most powerful when your **inner union is aligned.**

Spiritual Affirmation:

"I honor the divine masculine and divine feminine within me. I create from balance. I rise from unity. I walk as wholeness in all things."

LAW 4 – THE 42 DIVINE DECLARATIONS

Intro: The Sacred Confessions of Accountability & Alignment

"I have not lied. I have not stolen. I have not cursed the gods. I have not polluted the waters. I have not acted with evil intent."

These are not casual words. They are ancient keys of power — known as the **42 Divine Declarations,** or the **Negative Confessions of Ma'at**. They come from the *Papyrus of Ani,* what modern scholars call the "Egyptian Book of the Dead" — though in truth, it was the **Book of Life,** a guide for the soul's journey through eternity.

What Are the 42 Divine Declarations?

These declarations were spoken by the deceased in the **Hall of Ma'at,** where the soul was judged not by religion or belief, but by **character**. The soul's heart was weighed on a scale against the **feather of Ma'at** — the symbol of truth, justice, and divine order.

Before the weighing, the soul would proclaim 42 statements — declaring innocence of specific spiritual, social, and natural violations. These were not just for death — they were **meant to be practiced daily in life.**

They are not rules. They are reflections. They are spiritual accountability in action.

The Real Foundation Behind the Ten Commandments

Most of the so-called Ten Commandments in the Bible **originated from these 42 confessions.** Moses, raised and educated in Kemet, received wisdom that was already ancient. But while the commandments are **external laws,** the 42 Declarations are **internal spiritual affirmations** — they call the soul to speak on behalf of its own truth.

The Purpose of These Declarations

38

- To live in **alignment with Ma'at**

- To hold yourself accountable for your words, thoughts, and actions

- To maintain **spiritual integrity and balance**

- To **purify the soul daily**

- To remember that divine judgment is not punishment — it is **measuring your alignment with truth**

Why They're Called "Negative Confessions"

The word "negative" here doesn't mean bad — it means **negating what you have done wrong.** You are declaring:

"I have not harmed..."

"I have not dishonored..."

"I have not stolen..."

This is not self-righteousness — it is spiritual *self-review.*

Every time you say these declarations, you're tuning your soul to the vibration of righteousness, balance, and ancestral truth.

How We Will Break This Down

We will now go through **each of the 42 declarations:**

- Original statement

- Spiritual interpretation

- How it applied in ancient times

- How to apply it today

- Daily affirmation

This will make the Declarations **living principles**, not dead scripture.

DECLARATION 1

"I have not committed sin."

(Kemetic: "N ukheru en neb" – "I have not done wrong.")

Spiritual Interpretation:

This declaration speaks to the **foundational principle of Ma'at:** alignment. "Sin" in the Kemetic context was not about violating a religious code — it was about creating **imbalance, disharmony, or violation of divine order**.

To "not commit sin" meant that you had:

- Not acted against truth

- Not knowingly caused harm

- Not moved out of divine balance

In Kemet, morality was **measured by Ma'at,** not by arbitrary rules. You were responsible for knowing when your actions, thoughts, or words were **off-frequency** — and correcting them.

Ancient Meaning in Practice:

- Citizens were not judged by belief, but by **their effect on others and the community**

- Scribes, priests, and elders were expected to live as examples of Ma'at — justice, humility, truth

- Even in the smallest actions — trade, speech, parenting, leadership — one was expected to walk in divine integrity

Modern Application:

Today, we must return to this personal accountability. To say "I have not committed sin" is not to claim perfection — it is to commit to walking in alignment.

Ask yourself daily:

Have I done anything that violated truth, balance, or justice?

Did I speak from ego, fear, or manipulation?

Did I dishonor myself, my ancestors, or the universal laws?

This is not about guilt — it's about **awareness**. You cannot correct what you don't confront.

How to Practice It:

- Take 5 minutes daily to reflect: Did I stay aligned today?

- If you recognize imbalance, speak truth over yourself and correct it with action

- Use this declaration as a **reset**, a moment of **spiritual calibration**

Spiritual Affirmation:

"I walk in Ma'at. I honor truth in all things. I align my thoughts, words, and actions with divine order. I reject imbalance. I walk clean."

DECLARATION 2

"I have not committed robbery with violence."

(Kemetic: "N ukhem en setkem.")

Spiritual Interpretation:

This is not just about stealing — it's about **taking what is not yours** by **force,** manipulation, or intimidation. In Kemet, robbery with violence was not only a physical crime, but also a **spiritual violation of Ma'at**, because it disrupted **peace, justice**, and **harmony**.

Violence included not only physical aggression, but also:

- **Coercion**

- **Abuse of power**

- **Emotional or economic manipulation**

- **Spiritual bullying** — using fear to control

To rob another — of peace, safety, dignity, or resources — was a direct offense against Ma'at.

Ancient Meaning in Practice:

- In Kemet, justice was not about punishment but restoring balance

- If you took something by force, you were expected to **return and repair**

- Leaders and citizens alike were held to this standard — even pharaohs

- Violence disrupted social order and spiritual purity — it was considered a **pollution of the land**

Modern Application:

Today, we must ask:

- Have I taken anything through manipulation, threats, or dominance?

- Have I robbed someone of peace by my words, energy, or presence?

- Have I abused a position of power to control others?

This is not only about breaking into homes — it's about **breaking into someone's life** and causing harm through fear or force.

How to Practice It:

- Apologize and make amends if you've ever dominated someone

- Check your **tone and presence** — are you overpowering or disrespectful?

- Choose **restoration over revenge**, peace over power

- Refuse to support systems that **rob others of their voice, freedom, or resources**

When you walk in Ma'at, you are a protector, not a predator.

Spiritual Affirmation:

"I take nothing that is not mine. I honor the peace of others. I move without force, and I build without fear. I am a guardian of balance."

DECLARATION 3

"I have not stolen."

(Kemetic: "N ukhem.")

Spiritual Interpretation:

To steal is to **take without consent or right** — not just objects, but also **time, energy, credit, ideas, or opportunities**. In the spiritual law of Ma'at, stealing disrupts universal balance because it removes what has not been earned or aligned with.

This declaration affirms a life of **respect, discipline, and energetic integrity.** It teaches that **everything has a source**, and when you violate that source, you violate the divine order behind it.

Ancient Meaning in Practice:

- In Kemet, stealing wasn't just a material offense — it was a sign of **spiritual immaturity**

- Citizens were taught to **ask, trade, or create** — never to take

- Stealing was seen as a violation of **reciprocity** and the **natural flow of abundance**

- Even the act of **withholding** (like knowledge or fairness) could be viewed as stealing

Modern Application:

Stealing today takes many forms:

- Taking someone's **intellectual property** and claiming it as your own

- Wasting people's **time and energy** without purpose or permission

- **Cutting spiritual corners** — trying to skip the work and receive the reward

- Abusing **resources** that are meant to be shared (e.g., community benefits, trust, support)

To walk in Ma'at is to live a life where **nothing is taken by force, and everything is gained by truth.**

How to Practice It:

Be honest about what you've earned and what you haven't

Give credit where it's due — **honor the sources** of your wisdom, success, and inspiration

Pay for what you benefit from

Return what doesn't belong to you — physically, emotionally, spiritually

Create your own — the universe supports those who **produce, not poach**

When you refuse to steal, the universe opens the floodgates of authentic provision.

Spiritual Affirmation:

"I am a vessel of integrity. I take nothing that is not mine. I honor every exchange. I receive through alignment, not deception."

DECLARATION 4

"I have not slain men or women."

(Kemetic: "N ushet senenet.")

Spiritual Interpretation:

This declaration speaks not only against **physical murder**, but also against **spiritual, emotional, mental, and social harm** that can "kill" a person's spirit, dignity, or purpose.

In Ma'at, to "slay" someone wasn't limited to taking life. It included:

- **Destroying someone's reputation**

- **Crushing their spirit with words or control**

- **Public humiliation or betrayal**

- **Killing opportunities through envy or sabotage**

The ancient Kemetic understanding of life was holistic — **the soul could be wounded,** not just the body.

Ancient Meaning in Practice:

- To harm another unjustly was seen as a **direct attack on the divine spark within them**

- Even accidental or emotional harm was expected to be **acknowledged and repaired**

- The justice system focused on **restoration, not revenge**

- The emphasis was not only on what you did — but **what you allowed, supported, or ignored**

Modern Application:

This law applies deeply to how we treat each other today.

Ask yourself:

- Have I **killed someone's trust** through dishonesty?

- Have I **crushed someone's voice or confidence** with my words?

- Have I been silent while someone was **unjustly harmed?**

Even **neglect** or indifference in moments of injustice can spiritually slay another person.

How to Practice It:

- Be intentional with your words — they can heal or destroy

- Stop gossiping — it assassinates people who are not present to defend themselves

- Choose to build, not break

- If you've harmed someone's spirit, apologize, atone, and correct the pattern

- Stand up when others are being torn down — silence is agreement

Ma'at calls you to **be a protector of life**, not a participant in its destruction.

Spiritual Affirmation:

"I am a guardian of life and truth. I do no harm to others in body, mind, or spirit. My words heal. My presence uplifts. I am aligned with sacred protection."

DECLARATION 5

"I have not defrauded offerings."

(Kemetic: "N ukheset hetep.")

Spiritual Interpretation:

To "defraud offerings" means to **steal, withhold, misuse, or misrepresent something sacred**. In Kemet, offerings were not just physical gifts to the gods — they were **acts of devotion, energy, gratitude, and alignment**. Defrauding an offering meant you were:

- Giving with wrong intentions

- Withholding something sacred that should be shared

- Taking what was meant for divine use and misusing it for personal gain

- Offering something outwardly, but not inwardly

This declaration is about **integrity in your relationship with the Divine.** It's about **clean intentions, pure heart, and honest energy** behind your spiritual practices.

Ancient Meaning in Practice:

- Offerings included **bread, water, incense, prayer, service, and devotion**

- Temples functioned as spiritual power stations — they ran on clean offerings, not manipulation

- Priests were **judged more by purity of intent than material wealth**

- Misusing offerings could spiritually defile not just the temple, but the land and the people

Modern Application:

Today, "defrauding offerings" shows up when:

- People pray but don't mean it

- Leaders abuse tithes, donations, or spiritual trust

- We offer "time" to spiritual work, but spend it scrolling or gossiping

- We say we're giving love or support, but we're secretly judging or manipulating

To walk in Ma'at is to **offer with truth** — not performance. Every offering should come from a heart of honor.

How to Practice It:

- Be intentional in your prayers, meditations, and rituals — don't go through motions

- If you promise something to your ancestors, spirit, or community — **fulfill it**

- Offer your time, energy, and resources **purely, not for praise**

- Don't use spiritual language to mask personal agendas

- Treat your gifts (money, food, words) as sacred offerings — they carry frequency

Offerings are not just about what you give — they are about **how you give it.**

Spiritual Affirmation:

"I offer from a pure place. My giving is sacred, my service is sincere. I do not withhold from the divine, and the divine does not withhold from me."

DECLARATION 6

"I have not stolen from the gods."

(Kemetic: "N ukhesef netcheru.")

Spiritual Interpretation:

This declaration is about **respecting divine property, divine energy, and divine purpose.** In Kemet, the "gods" (netcheru) represented **aspects of nature, universal forces, and divine order** — not idols to be worshipped, but sacred powers to be honored and worked with.

To "steal from the gods" meant:

- **Taking what is sacred for selfish use**

- **Using spiritual gifts without acknowledging the source**

- **Claiming glory for what was given by divine will**

- **Blocking or misdirecting energy that was meant for a higher cause**

It is a declaration of **humility, accountability, and divine stewardship.**

Ancient Meaning in Practice:

- Temples were stocked with sacred items — food, incense, sacred tools — stealing from them was seen as a **cosmic offense**

- Priests were trusted not only to guard the offerings, but to **honor the spiritual contracts behind them**

- Power was seen as divine property — it wasn't yours to misuse or claim without responsibility

Modern Application:

In today's world, "stealing from the gods" looks like:

- Using your **gifts** without honoring the source — ancestors, spirit, Ma'at

- Claiming **spiritual knowledge or power** without living in integrity

- Misusing your **influence or platform** for ego, profit, or manipulation

- Ignoring your **calling** — keeping your light hidden, or refusing to serve when called

Everything you've been given — your mind, your talent, your voice, your vision — is on loan from the divine. To steal it is to **use it for self only.**

How to Practice It:

- Give credit to the divine for your breakthroughs, blessings, and wisdom

- Use your gifts **in alignment** with spiritual truth

- If you teach, speak, or lead — do it with **honor and responsibility**

- Don't suppress your calling — share your light

- Acknowledge that you are a **vessel**, not the source

When you give back to the divine, the divine multiplies everything in your life.

Spiritual Affirmation:

"I honor the divine within me. I use my gifts with humility. I am a vessel of Ma'at, and I serve with gratitude and truth."

DECLARATION 7

"I have not told lies."

(Kemetic: "N udjed medu.")

Spiritual Interpretation:

This declaration affirms that **truth is sacred** — not just in words, but in **energy, intent, and expression**. In the way of Ma'at, a lie is not just a false statement — it is **any distortion of reality,** especially when used to deceive, manipulate, or avoid responsibility.

To lie is to **create imbalance**, to break trust, and to mislead the flow of divine order. Truth is not always comfortable — but it is **always powerful.**

Ancient Meaning in Practice:

In Kemet, truth (Ma'at) was a **pillar of civilization** — judges, scribes, and priests were expected to be "true of voice" (Ma'at kheru)

To be caught in a lie was seen as a **spiritual flaw**, not just a moral issue

Speaking truth wasn't only about facts — it meant **aligning your speech with the frequency of divine law**

Lies were considered a form of **spiritual pollution** — they corrupted the heart and disrupted justice.

Modern Application:

Today, lies are normalized. But in Ma'at, even **small distortions** carry spiritual weight:

- Telling half-truths to avoid discomfort

- Lying to yourself about your calling, wounds, or potential

- Speaking falsely to gain status, sympathy, or control

- Using spiritual language to cover manipulation

- Living in truth is not about perfection — it's about **alignment**.

How to Practice It:

- Speak with integrity — even when it's hard

- If you've lied, **correct it and realign**

- Don't lie to yourself — truth starts inside

- Let your "yes" mean yes and your "no" mean no

- Avoid exaggeration, gossip, and flattery rooted in agenda

- If you're not ready to speak truth, be **silent instead of deceptive**

Remember: **Ma'at lives in your words.** Speak as if the universe is listening — because it is.

Spiritual Affirmation:

"My words are sacred. I speak in alignment with truth. I reject falsehood, manipulation, and distortion. I am Ma'at kheru — true of voice."

DECLARATION 8

"I have not carried away food."

(Kemetic: "N ushet khenfu.")

Spiritual Interpretation:

This declaration is not just about taking physical food — it is about **violating sacred provision, hoarding what should be shared, and disrupting the natural flow of nourishment.**

In Kemet, food was **not just sustenance** — it was a sacred substance. To unjustly take or withhold it was to violate **reciprocity, justice, and care for others**. Every loaf, every harvest, every offering was part of a divine ecosystem.

Ancient Meaning in Practice:

- Food offerings in temples were considered **gifts to the gods, ancestors, and community**

- To steal or take food that was **meant for someone else —** especially the poor, sick, or sacred spaces — was seen as a violation of Ma'at

- Sharing food was a spiritual act, part of healing, community, and ancestral reverence

- Feeding others was viewed as a direct **extension of divine service**

Modern Application:

Today, this law challenges how we:

- **Withhold resources** while others suffer

- Take advantage of **programs, donations, or assistance** not meant for us

- **Waste food** while others are hungry

- Use food, money, or aid as a **control tactic**

- Eat in ways that disrespect the **sacredness of the body or the Earth**

To "carry away food" can also mean consuming without gratitude, taking without acknowledging the **life force behind the meal.**

How to Practice It:

- Give when you can — **sharing food is a sacred offering**

- Say a word of gratitude before you eat — honor the divine exchange

- Do not take what was meant for someone else — whether food, opportunity, or energy

- Support access to food and resources for the undernourished

- Treat your body like a temple — don't pollute it with low-vibration foods

- Food is life — but in Ma'at, life must always be honored and shared.

Spiritual Affirmation:

"I honor divine provision. I receive with gratitude and give with love. I do not withhold what sustains others. I nourish in balance."

DECLARATION 9

"I have not uttered curses."

(Kemetic: "N uau medu.")

Spiritual Interpretation:

To "utter curses" is to speak words that carry **harmful, hateful, or destructive energy** — whether toward others, yourself, or the divine. In the spiritual system of Ma'at, words are **sacred tools** that carry **frequency, intention**, and **consequences**.

A curse is not always a spell or ritual — it can be:

- **A slanderous word**

- **A hateful comment**

- **A self-condemning thought**

- **Gossip, mockery, or verbal harm**

When you speak out of bitterness, jealousy, or ego, you project a frequency that disrupts Ma'at — and you **become accountable for what you release.**

Ancient Meaning in Practice:

- In Kemet, the tongue was seen as a **spiritual weapon** — it could build or destroy

- "Uttering curses" **included speaking falsely, emotionally, or spitefully**

- The concept of being "Ma'at kheru" (true of voice) required that your speech **uplift, align,** or **correct — never curse**

- Cursing the gods, the ancestors, or the innocent was seen as a major spiritual offense

Words were understood to be **living forces** — once released, they could not be taken back.

Modern Application:

Today, this declaration reminds us to check:

- What we say **behind closed doors**

- What we post online or speak over others

- The way we **talk to ourselves** in pain or failure

- Whether our "truth" is rooted in **healing or harm**

You don't have to use profanity to curse — every word that tears someone down, or poisons the atmosphere, carries that weight.

How to Practice It:

- Speak intentionally — pause before reacting

- If you've cursed someone in anger — clear the energy, make peace

- Refuse to gossip — it's **cursing by disguise**

- Speak to others as if their spirit is listening — because it is

- Use your words to **bless, uplift, teach, correct, or affirm**

Ma'at **lives in your tongue**. Speak in a way that heaven would echo.

Spiritual Affirmation:

"I use my voice for truth, not harm. My words carry light. I curse no one — not even myself. I speak only what uplifts and aligns."

DECLARATION 10

"I have not committed adultery."

(Kemetic: "N uar khet.")

Spiritual Interpretation:

This declaration is about **honoring divine union, respecting sacred agreements,** and living in sexual, emotional, and energetic integrity. In Ma'at, adultery was not just a physical act — it was a **spiritual betrayal**. It meant disrupting the harmony of trust, **violating sacred covenants,** and acting from **desire without discipline.**

Adultery in Kemetic wisdom included:

- Breaking trust in a committed bond

- Interfering in someone else's spiritual or marital union

- Using intimacy to manipulate, dominate, or deceive

- Engaging in sexual energy **without spiritual responsibility**

Ancient Meaning in Practice:

- Marriage in Kemet was a **spiritual agreement,** not just a social contract

- Fidelity was tied to **balance, legacy, and energetic alignment**

- Betrayal of union was seen as a **violation of Ma'at,** not just a moral failure

- **Women and men were both accountable** for protecting sacred union

More than shame or control, this law protected the **energetic** order of families, communities, and destiny paths.

Modern Application:

Today, this law speaks to:

- **Honoring your commitments** in romantic, spiritual, or covenant relationships

- Avoiding third-party interference in sacred bonds

- Practicing **sexual discipline and clarity** — not just chemistry

- Understanding that every union you enter creates energetic exchange

- Choosing **truth and transparency** over pleasure at the cost of integrity

In the spirit of Ma'at, intimacy is sacred — it should be **free, truthful, and aligned,** not secretive or self-serving.

How to Practice It:

- Be honest about your intentions — before committing your body or your word

- Don't participate in secrets — protect sacred space

- Know that **what you build dishonestly will crumble**

- Hold others accountable for how they treat sacred commitments

- If you've violated a bond — **seek restoration and inner repair**

This law calls us to treat love, union, and intimacy as **spiritual territory** — not just emotional escape

Spiritual Affirmation:

"I honor the sacred bonds I enter. I do not betray trust. I align my desires with divine order. My intimacy is sacred. My love is true."

DECLARATION 11

"I have not made anyone cry."

(Kemetic: "N ushet seshemu.")

Spiritual Interpretation:

This declaration speaks to **compassion, empathy, and accountability** for the emotional impact we have on others. In Ma'at, to cause someone to cry **unjustly** — through cruelty, betrayal, neglect, or humiliation — was to create **spiritual imbalance.**

This wasn't about avoiding all tears (since some tears bring healing), but about not **causing harm that leads to unnecessary suffering.**

It reminds us: **people's spirits are sacred,** and when we wound them with our actions, words, or silence, we become responsible for that pain.

Ancient Meaning in Practice:

- Emotional harm was not taken lightly in Kemet — especially toward the **vulnerable**, like children, the poor, or the elderly

- Justice included **repairing emotional damage,** not just physical or material violations

- Leaders were expected to **protect peace,** not provoke pain

- To make another cry unjustly disrupted not only Ma'at — it was considered a **curse upon the soul** unless repented and repaired

Modern Application:

Today, this declaration calls us to check:

- How we speak in **anger, sarcasm, or ego**

- Whether we cause harm and then **dismiss the effect**

- How our emotional immaturity may cause **harm to others' hearts**

- The ways we may have **gaslit, abandoned, betrayed, or shamed others**

It also asks: *Have I made myself cry by abandoning my own truth or betraying my own soul?*

How to Practice It:

- Apologize to anyone you've caused pain — especially if it was **intentional or avoidable**

- Be mindful of how your presence, power, or words affect others

- Hold space when others are vulnerable — don't add salt to their wounds

- Don't weaponize emotions — yours or others'

- **Heal your own pain**, so you don't bleed it onto others

Compassion is a spiritual technology. When practiced, it creates ripple effects of healing.

Spiritual Affirmation:

"I am a healer, not a harmer. I speak with care, act with compassion, and leave others better than I found them. I do not add pain to the world — I restore peace."

DECLARATION 12

"I have not felt sorrow without reason."

(Kemetic: "N uaa renen.")

Spiritual Interpretation:

This declaration is about **emotional mastery** — not suppression. In Ma'at, sorrow was natural and sacred when aligned with truth. But to dwell in sorrow **without cause**, or to make sorrow a habit without reflection, was considered a form of **spiritual imbalance.**

The law reminds us that sorrow, when left unchecked or unexamined, can become **self-inflicted suffering,** emotional manipulation, or a detachment from gratitude and purpose.

This isn't about denying pain — it's about **not feeding it when there is no root.**

Ancient Meaning in Practice:

- Emotional health was a core part of spiritual alignment in Kemet

- Grief and sorrow were honored — but processed through **rituals, song, dance, tears, and offerings**

- People were not shamed for sorrow — but were guided through it

- Chronic sadness without cause was believed to block **divine flow and inner light**

This declaration protected against **emotional stagnation** — the kind that distracts, drains, and disconnects.

Modern Application:

Today, this declaration reminds us:

- To distinguish between **sacred sorrow** and **emotional patterns we haven't confronted**

- That sometimes we feel sorrow because of **energy we've absorbed,** not because something is wrong

- That sorrow can also be a **spiritual awakening** — but must be met with clarity and care

It also calls us to ask:

Am I using sorrow to avoid truth, to gain sympathy, or to stay small?

How to Practice It:

- Journal your feelings — ask: *Where is this sorrow coming from?*

- Don't suppress sadness — but seek the **root and meaning**

- Don't let sorrow become your identity — release, realign, and rise

- Choose gratitude as a healing tool — it's the vibration that gently clears sorrow

- If your sorrow has no name — fast, pray, and cleanse until clarity comes

Ma'at teaches emotional honesty — not emotional bondage.

Spiritual Affirmation:

"I honor sacred sorrow, but I do not live in it without cause. My heart is open to healing. I allow joy and gratitude to rise where sadness once lived."

DECLARATION 13

"I have not assaulted anyone."

(Kemetic: "N ukhesef remet.")

Spiritual Interpretation:

This declaration affirms your commitment to **nonviolence, self-control, and sacred conduct.** To "assault" someone in the way of Ma'at doesn't only mean physical harm — it includes:

- **Verbal attacks**

- **Energetic aggression**

- **Emotional manipulation or domination**

- Any form of **violation that disturbs another's peace or safety**

This is a reminder that every person is a divine being, and to harm them is to harm the **divine reflection within them — and within yourself.**

Ancient Meaning in Practice:

In Kemet, assault was considered a breach of **divine law, not just civil law**

Emotional outbursts, physical abuse, or intimidating others broke the flow of Ma'at

Warriors were trained not only in skill, but in discipline and spiritual restraint

The goal was not just peacekeeping — but **energetic responsibility** for how one's presence impacted others

Modern Application:

Assault today can come in subtle forms:

- Raising your voice to intimidate

- Constantly criticizing to control

- Pressuring others with fear or guilt

- Physically violating space, consent, or boundaries

It also asks: *Have I assaulted myself?* — through shame, neglect, or inner violence.

How to Practice It:

- Practice **calm in conflict** — choose response over reaction

- Speak truth without attacking

- Respect people's physical, spiritual, and emotional boundaries

- Don't dominate — **create space for mutual safety and power**

- Apologize and correct if you've ever harmed someone, even unknowingly

The way you handle power is a reflection of your alignment with Ma'at.

Spiritual Affirmation:

"I am a keeper of peace. I do no harm in word, thought, or deed. My presence is safe, my heart is clear, and my strength is rooted in restraint."

DECLARATION 14

"I have not been deceitful."

(Kemetic: "N udjed djedu.")

Spiritual Interpretation:

To be deceitful is to **intentionally distort the truth, conceal your true intentions,** or **present a false image** to gain advantage or avoid accountability. In the system of Ma'at, deceit was not merely lying — it was a violation of trust, a form of spiritual fraud.

This declaration reminds us that **deceit creates energetic debt.** When your words or actions mislead others — even subtly — you pull yourself out of alignment with divine truth.

Ancient Meaning in Practice:

- In Kemet, spiritual leaders, scribes, and judges were expected to be **"true of voice" (Ma'at kheru)**

- Deceit was considered a **form of darkness,** a poison that disrupted relationships, justice, and communal order

- Even **silent deceit** — misleading without speaking — was condemned

- The ancients believed **your spirit could not evolve if it carried dishonesty**

Modern Application:

Deceit today may look like:

- Pretending to be one thing while hiding another

- Giving false impressions to gain influence or avoid judgment

- Withholding key information in a way that **leads others off course**

- Hiding behind spirituality, kindness, or business while operating with manipulation or hidden agendas

This declaration calls you to **radical transparency** — not for perfection, but for **purity of intent.**

How to Practice It:

- Be clear with your intentions — in relationships, work, and service

- Don't say "I'm good" when you're not — **emotional deceit is still deceit**

- Speak your truth, even if it's uncomfortable — **truth creates clean alignment**

- Stop performing — show up **authentically**, even if imperfectly

- If you've deceived, don't hide — **repair, realign, and return to Ma'at**

Ma'at is not about performance — it is about **pure presence.**

Spiritual Affirmation:

"I live in honesty. I do not deceive with words, silence, or masks. I speak what is true. I walk in transparency. I trust that truth is always enough."

.

DECLARATION 15

"I have not stolen land."

(Kemetic: "N ukheset ta.")

Spiritual Interpretation:

To steal land is to **violate the sacred relationship between people, Earth, and divine order**. In Ma'at, land was not just property — it was **ancestral ground, spiritual territory, and living energy** tied to the Creator and the community.

This declaration affirms that you have not:

- Taken what belongs to another

- **Displaced others for your own gain**

- Violated boundaries without permission or alignment

- Treated sacred ground as personal possession

It's also about **respecting your own ground** — not allowing yourself to be uprooted from your purpose, lineage, or mission.

Ancient Meaning in Practice:

- In Kemet, land was given as inheritance from ancestors and the divine — to misuse it was to dishonor **both**

- Land theft was considered one of the **gravest crimes**, because it destroyed lives, families, and spiritual alignment

- Even borders and temple grounds were respected with **ceremonial boundaries and offerings**

- Every village had **ancestral land keepers** responsible for honoring the Earth and protecting rights

Modern Application:

Today, this law speaks to:

- Exploiting land, culture, or space that doesn't belong to you

- **Gentrification and displacement**

- Disrespecting burial sites, sacred ground, indigenous land, or community spaces

- Stealing **intellectual, spiritual, or creative land** — claiming territory you didn't earn or inherit

It also asks:

Are you protecting your spiritual land?

Or have you allowed someone to plant foreign seeds in your mind, your body, or your legacy?

How to Practice It:

- Acknowledge the history of the land you live on

- Give back when you've gained through privilege, access, or unearned space

- Set **clear energetic boundaries** — don't let others colonize your peace

- Honor your **ancestral inheritance,** whether physical, spiritual, or creative

- Don't claim what isn't yours — and don't let anyone steal what is

Land, like truth, must be honored, protected, and walked upon with reverence.

Spiritual Affirmation:

"I honor sacred ground. I do not take what is not mine — physically or spiritually. I protect my inheritance. I respect all boundaries, including my own."

DECLARATION 16

"I have not eavesdropped."

(Kemetic: "N ushetep seten.")

Spiritual Interpretation:

To eavesdrop is to **listen where you were not invited,** to **invade sacred space,** and to **intercept energy that was not meant for you.** In Ma'at, privacy and boundaries were deeply respected. To eavesdrop was seen as a form of **spiritual trespassing** — not just a lack of manners, but a violation of divine order.

Eavesdropping is rooted in **curiosity driven by distrust, insecurity, or control,** and it leads to **false judgment, unnecessary conflict, or toxic gossip.**

Ancient Meaning in Practice:

- In Kemet, community and spiritual leaders were taught to **protect confidentiality and sacred conversation**

- Listening without permission was considered a **breach of integrity and honor**

- Respecting someone's voice meant also respecting **when and where** they chose to speak

70

- Wisdom was earned — not stolen through sneaking, spying, or invading privacy

Modern Application:

Today, eavesdropping shows up as:

- Listening to conversations not meant for you — physically or digitally

- **Spying on someone's social media,** texts, or messages without permission

- **Reading into private matters,** then misusing that knowledge

- Inserting yourself into conversations or spaces to gather information, not to bring healing

This law reminds us that **every voice deserves sacred space** — and **listening is a privilege**, not a right.

How to Practice It:

- Mind your frequency — don't go looking for what was not offered

- Build trust by respecting boundaries

- If you overhear something sensitive, **protect the energy,** don't spread it

- Don't feed your insecurity through surveillance — feed it through inner work

- Honor that every conversation has a **spiritual context** — and it's not always yours to witness

Ma'at teaches that **alignment requires discretion** — and that true power is often silent, not nosy.

Spiritual Affirmation:

"I protect sacred conversations. I do not violate privacy or peace. I trust what I need to know will be revealed to me in divine timing."

DECLARATION 17

"I have not misbehaved or acted with arrogance."

(Kemetic: "N urekh ekhet.")

Spiritual Interpretation:

This declaration affirms your commitment to **humility, spiritual maturity, and emotional self-control**. In the way of Ma'at, "misbehavior" was not just about disobedience — it referred to any conduct that was **disruptive, disrespectful, immature, or rooted in ego.**

Arrogance was especially dangerous — it reflected **false elevation**, where one believed themselves **above Ma'at**, above others, or beyond correction.

To walk in divine order, you must walk in **balance and awareness** — not entitlement.

Ancient Meaning in Practice:

In Kemet, even kings (Pharaohs) were expected to rule with humility — they were seen as **servants of Ma'at**, not gods over men

Arrogance was a sign of **spiritual instability** — a soul out of tune with divine purpose

Misbehavior toward elders, the temple, the community, or ancestors was considered a **breach of sacred trust**

Greatness was honored only when it was **grounded in service, not self-exaltation**

Modern Application:

This declaration challenges us to ask:

- Am I acting in **alignment or impulse?**

- Have I treated someone as beneath me?

- Do I reject correction out of ego?

- Do I **show off wisdom,** instead of living it with grace?

Arrogance isn't always loud — sometimes it hides in judgment, superiority, or spiritual pride.

How to Practice It:

- **Slow down your reactions** — don't act out of impulse or dominance

- Stay teachable — **no matter how much you know**

- Serve without needing recognition

- Let your actions speak louder than your titles

- Reflect often: "Am I acting from **truth or ego?"**

Ma'at doesn't require perfection — but it demands **awareness of how your energy moves through the world.**

Spiritual Affirmation:

"I walk in humility. I am guided, not boastful. I choose grace over ego. I serve truth, not image. I am powerful and grounded."

DECLARATION 18

"I have not caused terror."

(Kemetic: "N ureth.")

Spiritual Interpretation:

To cause terror is to **intentionally incite fear**, chaos, or emotional instability in others. In the path of Ma'at, this is a serious spiritual offense — because fear disconnects people from their divine center. **Terror is spiritual theft:** it robs peace, clarity, and trust.

This declaration is not only about physical violence — it also speaks to:

- **Verbal threats or intimidation**

- **Manipulating others through fear**

- **Creating anxiety, dread, or panic for control**

- **Spreading destructive or chaotic energy unnecessarily**

Causing terror is the **antithesis of Ma'at**, which is rooted in safety, order, balance, and trust in divine protection.

Ancient Meaning in Practice:

- In Kemet, **leaders, warriors, and even parents** were held accountable for **how they used fear**

- The presence of a true servant of Ma'at was meant to **calm,** not **threaten**

- **Fear-based leadership**, sorcery, or manipulation was condemned as **dishonoring the gods and the ancestors**

  - Creating a climate of fear was seen as opening the gates to **Isfet** — chaos, disorder, and decay

Modern Application:

This law asks you to examine:

- Do I use fear to get others to do what I want?

- Have I **manipulated, threatened,** or **gaslit** someone emotionally?

- Do I leave people **spiritually shaken** instead of centered?

- Do I spread messages that inspire **panic, paranoia, or division?**

Sometimes terror is **loud and violent**. Other times it's **emotional and subtle** — but the impact is the same.

How to Practice It:

- Be mindful of the **atmosphere you create**

- Choose words that protect and empower — not weaken or frighten

- If you've caused someone to fear you, **repent and repair**

- Don't spread panic in conversation or online — speak truth, not hysteria

- Lead, teach, and love with **light, not pressure**

Ma'at calls for presence that is powerful — but never oppressive.

Spiritual Affirmation:

"I bring peace, not panic. I create calm, not confusion. My presence restores trust. I use my power with wisdom, not intimidation."

DECLARATION 19

"I have not overstepped my boundaries."

(Kemetic: "N ushen ren.")

Spiritual Interpretation:

This declaration affirms the principle of **spiritual and energetic boundaries** — a key tenet of Ma'at. To overstep your boundaries is to **enter territory that is not yours**, whether physically, emotionally, relationally, or spiritually. It's a violation of **respect, timing, and order.**

Boundaries are not about separation — they are about **alignment.** To honor them is to move in divine timing, in your own lane, and in your own purpose.

Ancient Meaning in Practice:

- In Kemet, physical land and sacred spaces had **defined limits** — entering without permission was seen as dishonorable

- Even in relationships, roles and hierarchies were **respected as divine assignments**

- Overreaching spiritually — trying to access knowledge or power not granted — was considered **dangerous and out of order**

- Humility and discipline kept society in Ma'at — **knowing your place wasn't weakness, it was wisdom**

Modern Application:

This law challenges us to reflect on:

- Times we've **inserted ourselves into matters** that didn't concern us

- Moments when we **pushed relationships, conversations, or outcomes too far**

- Situations where we **spiritually trespassed** — trying to guide, fix, or control what wasn't ours to handle

- The **importance of protecting your own energy** from being overstepped by others, too

Every person, space, and season has a divinely assigned perimeter. Crossing that without permission is a spiritual error.

How to Practice It:

- Respect others' timing, process, and space

- Ask before offering correction, help, or spiritual insight

- Be mindful of **emotional, physical, and energetic boundaries** in all relationships

- Guard your own sacred space — not everyone should have access to you

- Don't force **spiritual growth** — yours or others' — ahead of divine schedule

True power is knowing **when to step back** just as much as when to step forward.

Spiritual Affirmation:

"I honor sacred limits. I stay in divine alignment. I do not force, push, or trespass. I protect space — mine and others' — in truth and love."

DECLARATION 20

"I have not falsely accused anyone."

(Kemetic: "N udjed setem.")

Spiritual Interpretation:

To falsely accuse is to **speak against someone without truth,** evidence, or divine alignment. In Ma'at, this was not just a moral error — it was a **spiritual crime,** because it **distorted truth, damaged reputations,** and created **karmic debt.**

This declaration protects the **integrity of speech**, the **power of testimony,** and the sacred balance of justice.

Ancient Meaning in Practice:

- In Kemet, **judgment was sacred** — truth was verified through multiple levels of divine law, elder insight, and evidence

- A false accusation could bring serious consequences, not just to the accused but to the **accuser's spiritual record**

- Priests and judges were trained to **speak only after verifying the whole of a matter**

- Reputation was part of one's **spiritual identity** — to defame it falsely was to attack the divine within them

Modern Application:

This law is especially important today, where **gossip, slander, and social media** accusations spread rapidly — often without proof.

It asks:

- Have I spoken something about someone I **didn't verify?**

- Have I believed something without hearing both sides?

78

- Have I participated in **tearing someone down** without divine or factual clarity?

False accusations don't always come from malice — sometimes they come from **pain, projection, or assumption**. But the spiritual cost is the same.

How to Practice It:

Always seek truth — not just emotional reaction

Never speak publicly about someone's character **without verification and alignment**

Be cautious when sharing information — "Did I see it, or did I hear it?"

Refuse to join conversations that **judge without justice**

If you've falsely accused or participated in it — repent, correct, and repair

Ma'at teaches that **speech is sacred testimony** — don't offer it carelessly.

Spiritual Affirmation:

"I speak with integrity. I do not judge without truth. I protect the innocent. I reject distortion. My words honor justice and balance."

DECLARATION 21

"I have not been angry without cause."

(Kemetic: "N uren en khef.")

Spiritual Interpretation:

This declaration speaks to the sacred discipline of **emotional regulation**. In Ma'at, anger was not forbidden — but it was to be **righteous, measured, and aligned with divine justice.** To be angry without cause is to allow **ego, trauma, or imbalance** to rule your spirit.

Unjustified anger creates harm, chaos, and misjudgment. Righteous anger brings correction and truth. This law reminds us that **feeling is natural — but reaction must be mastered.**

Ancient Meaning in Practice:

In Kemet, warriors and priests were trained in **emotional mastery** — power meant little without control

Anger used to **dominate**, shame, or manipulate others was considered a **spiritual violation**

Emotions were respected — but you were expected to reflect before reacting

The one who could not control their temper was seen as **out of alignment with Ma'at**

Modern Application:

This declaration asks:

- Am I triggered because of this moment — or because of something unhealed in me?

- Do I let anger turn into **verbal, emotional, or spiritual violence?**

- Have I harmed others with my tone, silence, or outbursts — only to realize later I had no true cause?

Anger that is misaligned becomes a **weapon of Isfet (chaos).** But anger that is rooted in truth can fuel **divine correction and accountability.**

How to Practice It:

- Pause when you feel anger rise — breathe, don't explode

- Ask yourself: Is this anger righteous, or is it wounded?

- If your anger was misdirected, **apologize and realign**

- Channel anger into **constructive change,** not destruction

- Don't judge yourself for feeling angry — but be accountable for what you do with it

Ma'at teaches that even your emotions must **bow to divine order.**

Spiritual Affirmation:

"I feel with awareness. I express with discipline. My anger serves truth, not ego. I am ruled by purpose, not impulse."

DECLARATION 22

"I have not seduced anyone's partner."

(Kemetic: "N uar anit.")

Spiritual Interpretation:

This declaration affirms your commitment to **respecting sacred unions, honoring emotional boundaries,** and walking in **sexual integrity**. In Ma'at, seduction was not only about physical desire — it was about **using charm, influence, or manipulation** to disrupt a spiritual bond.

To seduce someone's partner is to **violate trust**, create spiritual imbalance, and dishonor both **yourself and their union.**

Ancient Meaning in Practice:

In Kemet, relationships were understood as divine contracts —
forged not just by love, but by spiritual alignment and ancestral
guidance

Interfering in someone's union, even emotionally or energetically,
was viewed as spiritual sabotage

Seduction was not just physical — it included words, looks,
intentions, or manipulation

The breakdown of divine partnerships was seen as a threat to
family, order, and legacy

Modern Application:

This law asks:

- Have I sought attention from someone already committed?

- Have I emotionally or sexually entangled someone
  knowing they had obligations elsewhere?

- Have I enjoyed being desired by another while saying "I
  didn't do anything"?

- Have I encouraged or allowed a bond that wasn't aligned
  with truth?

Even if no act was committed — the **intention and energy matter.**
In Ma'at, **seduction is spiritual dishonor** if it violates covenant or
creates chaos.

How to Practice It:

- Stay grounded in self-worth — don't validate yourself by
  being desired by the unavailable

- Refuse to entertain romantic energy from those in relationships

- Don't feed emotional connections that belong to someone else

- Protect your energy — don't become the target or the tool of someone else's confusion

- Seek sacred love — not stolen moments

True divine union honors all parties involved — visible and unseen.

Spiritual Affirmation:

"I respect sacred unions. I do not violate trust for pleasure. I move in purity and divine timing. What is mine is aligned. What is not, I release in peace."

DECLARATION 23

"I have not polluted myself."

(Kemetic: "N usek nef.")

Spiritual Interpretation:

This declaration affirms your commitment to **inner cleanliness, spiritual purity**, and **self-respect**. In Ma'at, pollution was not limited to dirt or physical uncleanliness — it referred to anything that **corrupted your body, mind, spirit, or energy field.**

To pollute yourself is to:

- **Indulge in what you know weakens you**

- **Feed your spirit toxins — through people, substances, thoughts, or habits**

- **Diminish your divine frequency through misalignment**

It is not about shame — it is about **alignment, self-honor, and energetic hygiene.**

Ancient Meaning in Practice:

- In Kemet, purification rituals were daily — spiritual baths, anointing, fasting, and mental cleansing were standard

- Priests and initiates practiced **internal and external purification** before entering sacred space

- Pollution was treated not just as dirt, but as **any blockage between you and divine flow**

- It was understood that **your body is a temple**, and what you consume becomes your vibration

Modern Application:

This law challenges us to ask:

- Have I consumed food, media, substances, or energy that lower my vibration?

- Have I entangled with people or environments that **don't align with my divine path?**

- Do I neglect spiritual hygiene — not praying, fasting, cleansing, or recalibrating?

- Have I polluted my own name through self-betrayal?

Ma'at reminds us: **purity is not perfection — it's presence. It's choosing clarity over chaos.**

How to Practice It:

- Clean your body with intention — sacred baths, water, oil, herbs

- Clean your mind — fast from toxic thoughts, gossip, or media

- Clean your spirit — pray, meditate, reset

- Don't allow others to **dump energy into your temple**

- Speak kindly to yourself — your words are spiritual air

When you honor your temple, the divine takes residence within you.

Spiritual Affirmation:

"I am clean in thought, word, and being. I purify what enters my spirit. I do not pollute myself — I protect the sacred within me."

DECLARATION 24

"I have not terrorized anyone."

(Kemetic: "N unekh.")

Spiritual Interpretation:

This declaration calls you to walk in **peace, presence, and protective power.** To terrorize someone is to **intentionally instill fear,** to **disturb their peace,** or to become a source of **emotional, spiritual, or physical threat.**

In Ma'at, to be a terror was to be **out of alignment with divine order** — it meant that your presence created **harm instead of harmony, fear instead of faith, confusion instead of clarity.**

This applies not only to outward aggression, but also to:

- **Verbal intimidation**

- **Emotional volatility**

- **Manipulating others through fear or pressure**

Ancient Meaning in Practice:

- In Kemet, causing fear unjustly was a **violation of the cosmic balance**

- Leaders and elders were expected to **guide, not dominate**

- Even warriors had **codes of restraint** — they protected peace, not provoked fear

- A person who brought terror into the home or temple was considered **polluted and spiritually unstable**

Modern Application:

This law asks:

- Do others walk on eggshells around me?

- Have I made people feel unsafe, emotionally or spiritually?

- Have I used fear to control — even passively or subtly?

- Have I ignored the damage my energy **creates** when I am ungrounded?

You are called to be a **temple of light,** not a storm of anxiety.

How to Practice It:

- Speak with gentleness — especially in conflict

- Be aware of your presence — do you bring calm or confusion?

- Don't yell, threaten, or pressure others — even if you feel justified

- Create safe space — for children, elders, lovers, and even strangers

- Heal your inner chaos — so you don't spread it outward

When you walk in peace, you restore others by your presence alone.

Spiritual Affirmation:

"I am a safe place. I bring peace, not pressure. I walk with power that protects — not power that provokes. I calm the storm, I do not become it."

DECLARATION 25

"I have not disobeyed the law."

(Kemetic: "N usekheru.")

Spiritual Interpretation:

In the path of Ma'at, "law" is not limited to written statutes — it includes **divine order, natural principles, ancestral codes,** and **spiritual agreements**. This declaration affirms that you have lived in **alignment with sacred law**, not rebellion against it.

To disobey the law is to:

- Know what is right but **consciously violate it**

- Live by impulse instead of principle

- **Dismiss divine instruction** in favor of ego or convenience

This declaration is about **obedience to divine alignment**, not blind submission to systems of oppression. Ma'at's law is about **truth, balance, and responsibility** — not control.

Ancient Meaning in Practice:

- In Kemet, the law of Ma'at governed **everything from speech to leadership to land use**

- To violate spiritual law was to **pollute the land, dishonor the ancestors, and misalign the soul**

- Law was tied to **justice, community peace, and cosmic order** — not just punishment

- Obedience to Ma'at meant living by the principles of **truth, reciprocity, humility, and respect**

Modern Application:

This law invites deep reflection:

- Am I living in alignment with divine instruction — or avoiding it?

- Have I violated truth to protect my comfort?

- Do I reject spiritual guidance because it conflicts with what I "want"?

- Have I created my own rules to avoid **universal accountability?**

You are not expected to be perfect — but you are expected to **seek alignment,** and return quickly when you fall out of it.

How to Practice It:

- Study and meditate on the **Laws of Ma'at** and Universal Law

- Follow the guidance of spirit, even when it challenges your ego

- Keep your word — your promises are your personal laws

- Honor the systems that protect life, peace, and dignity — and challenge those that do not

- Walk in truth even **when it costs comfort** — it will return as freedom

True obedience is not submission — it's spiritual mastery.

Spiritual Affirmation:

"I walk in divine law. I obey truth, not trend. I live by principle, not pressure. Ma'at is my compass, and I stay aligned with its order."

DECLARATION 26

"I have not caused sorrow."

(Kemetic: "N usekem renen.")

Spiritual Interpretation:

This declaration affirms your commitment to being a **bringer of peace, not pain**. To cause sorrow is to knowingly or carelessly **inflict emotional or spiritual harm** on another — through actions, words, betrayal, or neglect.

In Ma'at, the soul is responsible not only for what it does, but for how it **affects the hearts of others.** To walk in divine order is to move with **awareness, gentleness,** and **compassion**, ensuring that your presence brings **healing, not heaviness.**

Ancient Meaning in Practice:

- In Kemet, causing unnecessary sorrow — especially to elders, children, or those under your care — was a sign of **disorder and ego**

- Emotional maturity was considered a form of **spiritual strength**

- Leaders and family heads were **trained in restraint** — so their words and choices would uplift, not break

- Causing sorrow without justice was seen as **dishonoring the divine spark in another**

Modern Application:

This law asks:

- Have I broken hearts without taking responsibility?

- Have I **dismissed or ignored** someone's emotional needs?

- Have I ever caused pain to prove a point, win a fight, or protect my pride?

- Have I planted seeds of sorrow in someone's life through dishonor, infidelity, or betrayal?

This does **not** mean never speaking truth or holding boundaries — it means not using your power to wound when you could **build or release with grace.**

How to Practice It:

- Be mindful of your emotional footprint

- Speak with clarity and care, especially during conflict

90

- Apologize quickly when you know you've hurt someone

- Leave people with peace — not lingering wounds

- Be someone whose presence helps others feel **safe, loved, and respected**

You are not responsible for everyone's feelings — but you are responsible for what **your energy contributes** to their journey.

Spiritual Affirmation:

"I do not add sorrow to the world. My words heal, my hands protect, my heart uplifts. I walk gently, speak truthfully, and leave others whole."

DECLARATION 27

"I have not acted with insolence."

(Kemetic: "N usekh tefu.")

Spiritual Interpretation:

To act with insolence is to move with **disrespect, arrogance, or contempt,** especially toward **elders, the divine, sacred laws, or others in authority or trust.** This declaration calls you to live in **humility, reverence, and self-awareness.**

In Ma'at, insolence is not just about rudeness — it's about **rejecting wisdom, mocking truth,** or refusing to **recognize order and honor**. It is the attitude of spiritual rebellion that places ego above alignment.

Ancient Meaning in Practice:

- In Kemet, **respect was foundational** — toward elders, ancestors, leaders, and even the land

- Acting with insolence toward the gods, rituals, or truth was seen as a **direct violation of Ma'at**

- Children were raised to honor **tone, posture, and presence,** not just obedience

- Arrogance was treated as a **spiritual flaw**, not just a social one

Modern Application:

This law asks:

- Have I **dismissed wisdom** because it came from someone I didn't respect?

- Have I dishonored others with my **tone, sarcasm, or pride?**

- Have I **rolled my eyes at correction,** even when I needed it?

- Have I mocked the sacred — even casually or playfully?

Insolence blocks blessings — because it closes the **heart and mind to divine instruction.**

How to Practice It:

- Speak to others the way you'd speak to your own ancestors

- Remain teachable — no matter how much you know

- Choose curiosity over criticism

- Correct without contempt

- When corrected, reflect first — then respond with maturity

- Ma'at teaches that strength walks with **honor**, not ego.

Spiritual Affirmation:

"I walk with respect and humility. I honor wisdom. I do not mock truth or dismiss guidance. I speak and act with grace, even in disagreement."

DECLARATION 28

"I have not stirred up strife."

(Kemetic: "N uded isfet.")

Spiritual Interpretation:

To stir up strife is to **intentionally create conflict, division, or chaos**, often through gossip, manipulation, envy, or instigation. In Ma'at, this is a serious offense — because **strife is a seed of Isfet (disorder)**, and those who spread it **weaken the bonds of family, community, and spiritual unity.**

This declaration is about being a **builder of peace,** not a **carrier of confusion.**

Ancient Meaning in Practice:

- In Kemet, creating conflict in the temple, household, or community was seen as a **spiritual violation,** not just a social one

- Those who **spread discord** were considered to be in service to **Isfet** — the opposite force of Ma'at

- Great emphasis was placed on **harmony, cooperation, and silent wisdom**

- Even when injustice was present, correction was expected to be handled with **order and discipline,** not chaos

Modern Application:

This law challenges us to reflect:

- Do I **fuel arguments** rather than solve them?

- Have I **shared information** that deepened division instead of healing it?

- Do I enjoy **watching conflict**, even if I didn't start it?

- Have I manipulated people against each other, or taken sides prematurely?

Strife is often rooted in **ego, jealousy**, or **woundedness**, but the result is always the same: **spiritual disorder.**

How to Practice It:

- Be a peacemaker — not a pot-stirrer

- Speak only when your words bring clarity, not conflict

- Don't take sides without truth

- Correct privately when possible — never to embarrass or dominate

- Use silence and presence to **diffuse energy**, not inflame it

Ma'at requires you to **protect peace like a sacred flame.**

Spiritual Affirmation:

"I do not stir conflict. I bring clarity, not confusion. I speak with peace, walk with wisdom, and build unity wherever I go."

DECLARATION 29

"I have not acted with undue haste."

(Kemetic: "N uhef em hesef.")

Spiritual Interpretation:

To act with undue haste is to **move without wisdom,** to **rush decisions,** or to **react before reflecting.** In Ma'at, such haste is seen as a form of **spiritual recklessness** — a failure to consult divine timing, discernment, or inner truth.

This declaration calls us to live with **intention,** not impulse — to move with **clarity, not chaos.**

Ancient Meaning in Practice:

- In Kemet, priests, scribes, and leaders were trained to **pause before responding,** to ensure they were aligned with Ma'at

- Rash behavior — whether in leadership, judgment, or warfare — was seen as a **sign of inner imbalance**

- Even sacred rituals followed **cosmic timing and precision** — to act before the appointed hour was to dishonor the divine

- Patience was considered a **virtue of the wise and spiritually mature**

Modern Application:

This law asks:

- Have I made decisions based on emotion instead of alignment?

- Have I spoken too quickly, acted without thought, or **reacted instead of reflected?**

- Do I **force timing,** instead of flowing with it?

- Have I failed to pray, journal, or seek guidance before taking action?

Spiritual haste often creates **unnecessary setbacks, confusion, and energetic debt.**

How to Practice It:

- Pause before major decisions — give space for spirit to speak

- Reflect before responding — even in conflict

- Don't confuse movement with momentum — **wait for alignment**

- Practice rituals of clarity: breathwork, **divination, silenceTrust that divine timing is always better than forced timing**

Ma'at teaches that **true power is not in speed — it is in precision.**

Spiritual Affirmation:

"I move in divine timing. I am not rushed by fear or ego. I pause, I listen, I align. What is for me will find me when I am ready."

DECLARATION 30

"I have not pried into others' matters."

(Kemetic: "N udjen neb.")

Spiritual Interpretation:

This declaration centers on the sacred law of **respecting privacy, boundaries, and divine timing.** To pry into others' matters is to **enter spiritual or personal territory uninvited** — whether out of curiosity, judgment, or control.

In Ma'at, every soul has its **own path, lessons, and timing**. To intrude without cause or permission is a form of **spiritual trespass** — and often rooted in ego rather than truth.

Ancient Meaning in Practice:

- In Kemet, privacy and discretion were marks of **wisdom and spiritual discipline**

- Scribes, healers, and leaders were taught to **observe without interfering**, unless divinely assigned to intervene

- Over-involvement was seen as **disrupting the natural process of growth,** karma, and accountability

- Respecting others' spiritual space was a **sacred form of honoring free will and divine unfolding**

Modern Application:

This law calls for deep self-reflection:

- Have I inserted myself into others' issues **without being asked?**

- Have I demanded answers or truth from someone who wasn't ready to share?

- Have I gathered information out of **nosiness**, not concern?

- Have I used spirituality to justify **spying, snooping, or confronting** others prematurely?

Spiritual maturity means knowing **when to step back as much as when to speak up**.

How to Practice It:

- Ask permission before advising, correcting, or investigating

- Don't pressure others to reveal what they're not ready to

- Trust that spirit reveals what you need to know — without chasing it

- Be curious about your own soul, not someone else's secrets

- Focus inward: *Where am I overreaching because I haven't healed or trusted?*

Ma'at teaches that **respecting another's space is an act of sacred humility.**

Spiritual Affirmation:

"I honor spiritual boundaries. I do not trespass into what is not mine. I trust divine timing, and I walk in respectful wisdom."

DECLARATION 31

"I have not multiplied words in speaking."

(Kemetic: "N udjed medu aani.")

Spiritual Interpretation:

This declaration speaks to the sacred law of **speech discipline**. To "multiply words" is to speak excessively, unnecessarily, or without

alignment — often diluting truth, creating confusion, or feeding ego.

In Ma'at, **every word carries vibration.** Speaking without purpose or intention was seen as **energetic pollution.** Silence was honored as wisdom. **Truth didn't need decoration** — only clarity and alignment.

Ancient Meaning in Practice:

- In Kemet, oracles, priests, and scribes were trained to speak **only when the words served truth**

- "Over-talking" or trying to dominate a space with words was seen as a **sign of imbalance or insecurity**

- The wise were known by their ability to **say little, but carry much power**

- Words were offerings — and to multiply them without care was to **disrespect the spirit of speech**

Modern Application:

This declaration asks:

- Do I speak just to fill silence — or to be heard and seen?

- Have I **over-explained,** trying to control how I'm perceived?

- Have I **gossiped**, ranted, or over-shared in ways that diluted my power?

- Do I confuse presence with performance?

Excessive talking often reflects an **unsettled heart or scattered spirit.**

How to Practice It:

- Pause before speaking — Does this need to be said?

- Let your words be **precise, potent, and peaceful**

- Practice silence as a sacred ritual

- Journal or pray before processing out loud with others

- Allow your presence to say more than your paragraphs

Ma'at teaches that **stillness holds more truth than sound when spirit is aligned.**

Spiritual Affirmation:

"I speak with clarity and purpose. I do not waste words. My silence holds power. My voice is sacred, and I use it wisely."

DECLARATION 32

"I have not harmed through speech."

(Kemetic: "N ushetep medu.")

Spiritual Interpretation:

This declaration affirms your responsibility to use **language as a tool for truth, healing, and clarity** — not for harm. In the divine order of Ma'at, speech is a **creative force**. Words don't just describe reality — they shape it.

To harm through speech is to use your voice to:

- **Wound, manipulate**, or **curse**

- Spread **gossip, slander, sarcasm**, or **verbal abuse**

- Speak **negativity into someone's life or into your own**

This declaration is about **disciplining your tongue** so that it becomes a channel of alignment — not destruction.

Ancient Meaning in Practice:

- In Kemet, words were considered **living energy** — once released, they could not be taken back

- Priests, scribes, and speakers were trained in **sacred speech,** where intention and vibration mattered

- Verbal harm was treated like spiritual assault — whether it was loud or subtle

- The tongue was believed to carry the power of **both healing and death**

Modern Application:

This law asks:

- Have I used my voice to cut others down — even in anger or "jokes"?

- Have I harmed someone's self-worth or joy with **reckless or reactive words?**

- Do I speak to manipulate, dominate, or "win" arguments?

- Have I spoken **destructive words over myself**, feeding fear, shame, or limitation?

What you say, you summon. Words carry **frequency, direction, and effect.**

How to Practice It:

- Pause before you speak — ask, *Is it true? Is it necessary? Is it kind?*

- If your words have wounded, take responsibility and seek repair

- Speak affirmations and blessings daily to **retrain your vocal vibration**

- Use your voice to uplift — even in correction

- Don't participate in **harmful dialogue** — in person or online

When you master your speech, you elevate your spirit.

Spiritual Affirmation:

"My words heal, not harm. I speak with power and grace. My voice is sacred, and I use it to build, bless, and align."

DECLARATION 33

"I have not acted with arrogance."

(Kemetic: "N usekhem.")

Spiritual Interpretation:

To act with arrogance is to move through the world with a **false sense of superiority,** believing yourself above others, above correction, or even above the divine. In Ma'at, arrogance is a **spiritual misalignment** — it disconnects you from truth, humility, and the ancestral flow of wisdom.

Arrogance shuts the ears, inflates the ego, and **blocks spiritual growth**. This declaration affirms a posture of **humility, honor, and reverence** — no matter how powerful, gifted, or knowledgeable you become.

Ancient Meaning in Practice:

- In Kemet, Pharaohs were seen as divine vessels — but were still expected to **serve Ma'at,** not self-glorify

- Arrogant behavior was considered **evidence of internal chaos** — and often led to downfall

- The wisest elders were the **quietest and most grounded,** not loud or boastful

- To walk in Ma'at meant to walk with **dignity, not dominance**

Modern Application:

This law asks:

- Do I secretly or openly feel **better than others?**

- Do I resist correction or feedback, assuming I already know?

- Have I used my status, knowledge, or position to **make others feel small?**

- Do I confuse confidence with **ego-driven inflation?**

There is a difference between **divine confidence and spiritual arrogance** — one attracts alignment, the other invites isolation.

How to Practice It:

- Approach each conversation with a willingness to learn

- Use your gifts to serve — not to self-promote

- Let others speak. Listen more than you correct

- Acknowledge your flaws as part of your sacred design

- Elevate others — not just yourself

Ma'at calls us to be vessels, not idols.

Spiritual Affirmation:

"I walk with grace, not ego. I am powerful and humble. I uplift without boasting. I serve without seeking glory. I am aligned with truth."

DECLARATION 34

"I have not schemed against others."

(Kemetic: "N udjen nesh.")

Spiritual Interpretation:

This declaration affirms your commitment to **truthful intent, transparent motives,** and **clean hands**. To scheme is to **plot in secret**, to **manipulate people or events for selfish gain,** often at the expense of others' trust, peace, or destiny.

In Ma'at, scheming is a form of **spiritual betrayal** — it shows that your mind and spirit are **working against the divine order,** not in alignment with it.

Ancient Meaning in Practice:

- The ancients believed that **your inner thoughts shape your outer world** — to plan harm, even silently, was to **pollute your own spiritual field**

- Scheming against others was associated with **Isfet,** the force of disorder and treachery

- Leaders, family members, and even scribes were judged not just by what they did, but by the **intention behind their actions**

- Ma'at required **purity of heart,** especially in dealings with others

Modern Application:

This law calls you to reflect:

- Have I manipulated outcomes to **benefit myself at another's expense?**

- Have I smiled in someone's face while plotting against them in secret?

- Have I withheld truth, created confusion, or stirred division for personal gain?

- Have I schemed even in thought — assuming it wouldn't matter if I didn't act?

Intent carries weight. The universe listens to the whispers of the heart.

How to Practice It:

- Be honest about your motives — even the ones that are hard to admit

- If you realize you've schemed, correct the harm and reset your alignment

- Refuse to participate in **backdoor conversations or power plays**

- Ask yourself often: Is my heart clean in this matter?

- Choose transparency, even if it feels risky — integrity always protects your path

Ma'at teaches that *what you build through deceit will crumble*, but what you build through truth will stand forever.

Spiritual Affirmation:

"I plan with purity. I intend no harm. I do not plot in shadows. My path is honest. My spirit is clean. My name is aligned with truth."

DECLARATION 35

"I have not slandered anyone."

(Kemetic: "N udjed mesyu.")

Spiritual Interpretation:

To slander is to speak **false, damaging, or dishonorable words** about another person with the intention (or carelessness) of **destroying their reputation, credibility, or peace.** In Ma'at, slander is a **double offense** — it wounds others while also **corrupting the speaker's spiritual integrity.**

This declaration affirms a life of **truthful speech, respect for others' names**, and a refusal to **weaponize words** for personal gain or emotional release.

Ancient Meaning in Practice:

- In Kemet, one's **name and reputation** were sacred — tied to their spiritual legacy

- To slander someone was not just socially wrong — it was considered an act of **energetic violence**

- False accusations, exaggerations, and dishonorable gossip were treated as serious offenses against Ma'at

- The title *Ma'at kheru* ("true of voice") was a spiritual honor — given only to those whose words **carried alignment, not harm**

Modern Application:

This law asks:

- Have I repeated **rumors** or **unconfirmed accusations?**

- Have I shared **damaging words** out of jealousy, anger, or insecurity?

- Have I told **truths with malicious intent**, knowing they would destroy someone's image?

- Have I participated in group conversations that tear others down behind their back?

You don't have to invent a lie to be guilty of slander — you just have to **distort or deliver truth without honor.**

How to Practice It:

- Refuse to speak on others if your words do not serve **healing, justice, or truth**

- If someone's name comes up, ask yourself: *Would I say this if they were here?*

- When tempted to speak negatively, **choose silence or redirection**

- Apologize and restore the reputation of anyone you've dishonored

- Protect others' names — even when they aren't protecting yours

Ma'at requires your words to be **pure offerings**, not poisoned arrows.

Spiritual Affirmation:

"I speak no slander. I protect the names of others. I do not distort, exaggerate, or destroy. My voice brings light — not shadows."

DECLARATION 36

"I have not exaggerated my words when speaking."

(Kemetic: "N udjed medu seshemu.")

Spiritual Interpretation:

This declaration speaks to the **integrity of speech**. To exaggerate is to **stretch the truth** — making something sound greater, worse, or more dramatic than it actually is. In Ma'at, exaggeration is seen as a form of **deception**, because it distorts reality and misleads others.

This law is about honoring **precision, truth, and spiritual maturity in how you express yourself.** Your words should **illuminate**, not **inflate**.

Ancient Meaning in Practice:

- In Kemet, exaggeration was viewed as a form of **dishonesty and imbalance** — a subtle break from Ma'at

- Those who spoke to impress, exaggerate, or embellish were considered **untrustworthy and immature**

- Speakers, scribes, and record-keepers were trained to **document and communicate with accuracy**

- The wise were valued not for how much they said — but for **how precisely** they expressed truth

Modern Application:

This law asks:

- Do I stretch the truth to get sympathy, attention, or validation?

- Do I **make stories more dramatic** just to be heard or believed?

- Have I **amplified someone's wrongs**, or **inflated my own accomplishments?**

- Do I confuse storytelling with **spiritual accuracy?**

When your words lack integrity, your **spiritual authority weakens** — even if others don't notice.

How to Practice It:

- Practice **truthful storytelling** — let the facts be enough

- Don't embellish your experiences or status to fit in or stand out

- Speak in a way that is **clear, not manipulative**

- Trust that your authentic truth carries more power than an inflated version ever could

- If you catch yourself exaggerating, correct it out loud — it builds trust and alignment

Ma'at teaches that **truth is already powerful** — it doesn't need inflation, only illumination.

Spiritual Affirmation:

"I speak clearly and truthfully. I do not stretch the truth for gain. My words are clean, balanced, and aligned. I trust that truth is enough."

DECLARATION 37

"I have not acted with evil intent."

(Kemetic: "N udjed isfet.")

Spiritual Interpretation:

This declaration centers on the **spiritual purity of intention.** In Ma'at, evil is not just what you do — it's the **energy behind what you do**. To act with evil intent is to knowingly move with **malice, jealousy, vengeance, or manipulation,** seeking to harm, control, or mislead others.

Even if the action seems small or subtle, if the intention is rooted in darkness, it carries **spiritual weight and karmic consequence.**

Ancient Meaning in Practice:

- In Kemet, intent was considered **just as important as outcome** — the gods and ancestors weighed the heart, not just the hands

- Ma'at was the force of **purity, truth, justice, and balance,** while Isfet represented **deception, disorder, and hidden wickedness**

- Evil intent wasn't measured only by physical harm — it included sowing doubt, disunity, or energetic harm

- Spiritual initiates were taught to **cleanse their thoughts and motives** before speaking, leading, or judging

Modern Application:

This law invites you to ask:

- Have I ever hoped for someone's downfall or pain — even silently?

- Have I **acted kindly while secretly wishing harm?**

- Have I used knowledge, charm, or influence to manipulate others?

- Have I justified impure intentions with **self-righteousness or revenge?**

Evil intent is often quiet — but the universe hears it clearly.

How to Practice It:

- Before you act, ask: Is my intention clean? Is this aligned with truth and peace?

- If you feel envy or resentment — pause, cleanse, and realign

- Repent for any harm you've desired, even if unspoken

- Use your spiritual tools (meditation, fasting, journaling) to clear emotional toxins

- Be honest with yourself — why you do something is as important as what you do

Ma'at teaches that **purity of heart is the beginning of all alignment.**

Spiritual Affirmation:

"I act with clean intention. I do not wish harm. My spirit is rooted in peace. My thoughts and actions are aligned with Ma'at."

DECLARATION 38

"I have not polluted the water."

(Kemetic: "N ushetep mu.")

Spiritual Interpretation:

Water in Ma'at is more than a natural element — it is a **sacred force**, a carrier of **life, memory, spirit,** and **cleansing power**. To pollute the water is to dishonor the flow of nature, to contaminate what sustains both body and soul.

This declaration speaks not only to physical pollution, but also to **spiritual and energetic** pollution — bringing toxicity into **spaces meant for renewal, healing, or nourishment.**

Ancient Meaning in Practice:

- In Kemet, the Nile was seen as **the bloodstream of the gods** — essential, sacred, and protected

- To dump waste, poison, or unclean offerings into the river was a **spiritual offense,** not just a civil one

- Water in temple rituals was used to **purify, bless, and initiate** — so polluting it symbolized profaning the sacred

- Initiates learned that **energy can be polluted, just like water** — and were taught to keep both clean

Modern Application:

This law asks:

- Have I **disrespected the Earth or natural resources** I depend on?

- Have I poured negativity into spaces meant for healing — homes, temples, relationships, or conversations?

- Have I ignored my role in keeping my own spirit, body, or surroundings clean and refreshed?

- Have I polluted spiritual waters with doubt, **bitterness, gossip, or trauma projection?**

Just as we keep water physically clean, we must protect **what flows within us and around us.**

How to Practice It:

- Avoid polluting water sources — even small acts of respect matter

- Cleanse your body and space with **intentional water** rituals (baths, libations, rain collection)

- Be mindful of what you pour into others — speak life, not poison

- Offer gratitude when using water — it responds to **frequency and prayer**

- Spiritually "filter" your energy before entering sacred spaces

Ma'at reminds us: **What you pour into the waters of life will return to you.**

Spiritual Affirmation:

"I honor the sacred flow. I keep the waters clean — within and around me. I do not bring poison into places of peace. I flow in purity and power."

DECLARATION 39

"I have not spoken scornfully."

(Kemetic: "N udjed hesy.")

Spiritual Interpretation:

To speak scornfully is to use your words with **contempt, mockery, belittlement, or superiority** — especially toward those who are vulnerable, different, or in positions of learning.

In Ma'at, scornful speech is a **spiritual offense** because it **destroys dignity, sows division,** and **feeds the ego.** It is not simply rude — it is **energetically violent,** especially when disguised as "joking," "truth-telling," or "tough love."

Ancient Meaning in Practice:

- The Kemetic spiritual tradition emphasized **measured, respectful speech** — even during disagreement

- Elders corrected with **compassion and clarity,** never ridicule

- Mocking the poor, the spiritually immature, or those walking a different path was seen as a sign of **inner weakness, not strength**

- Scornful tones were thought to **attract disharmony and curses**, even unintentionally

Modern Application:

This law invites you to ask:

- Have I **mocked others** for their appearance, beliefs, or struggle?

- Have I corrected with **shame instead of wisdom?**

- Have I scorned someone in private — or worse, in public — for clout or ego strokes?

- Have I directed **scornful speech inward**, speaking against my own spirit?

Scorn damages more than reputation — it **corrupts sacred connection** between souls.

How to Practice It:

- Speak to others as if they are **children of the divine** — because they are

- Choose correction that **restores**, not humiliates

- Let humility guide your tone, especially when you're in a position of power or knowledge

- Refuse to entertain or engage in **sarcasm and cruelty disguised as humor**

- Extend to others the same **grace and patience** you want when you're learning or growing

Ma'at teaches that your words either **build the temple or burn it down.**

Spiritual Affirmation:

"My speech uplifts. I do not scorn or shame. I speak with honor, even in correction. My words protect the dignity of all souls."

DECLARATION 40

"I have not cursed the gods."

(Kemetic: "N udjed neteru.")

Spiritual Interpretation:

To curse the gods is to show **disrespect, denial, or contempt** toward the divine forces that govern nature, spirit, and cosmic balance. In Ma'at, this is a direct violation of **sacred relationship** — dishonoring the very powers that sustain and protect life.

This declaration reminds us to **walk in reverence**, recognizing that the gods (Neteru) are not distant idols — they are **aspects of divine law,** reflected in nature, energy, ancestors, and even within ourselves.

Ancient Meaning in Practice:

- In Kemet, the Neteru were not "gods" in the Western sense — they were **principles of divine force:** truth (Ma'at), protection (Sekhmet), wisdom (Tehuti), creation (Ptah), and more

- Cursing or mocking the divine was seen as an act of **Isfet** — disrespecting order, power, and the ancestors

- Even doubt, sarcasm, or misuse of **sacred symbols was considered a breach of alignment**

- Devotion was expressed not just through ritual, but through **honor, gratitude, and humility**

Modern Application:

This law invites deep spiritual reflection:

- Do I speak against divine forces when life challenges me?

116

- Do I **mock spiritual practices or teachings** I don't understand?

- Do I **use the names of divine beings casually or without reverence?**

- Have I disconnected from the sacred because of trauma, bitterness, or disappointment?

Cursing the divine is often a symptom of **spiritual disconnection or ego pain** — not true rebellion.

How to Practice It:

- Reconnect with the divine forces in nature, your ancestors, and yourself

- Speak the names of the sacred with **intention and reverence**

- If you've cursed the gods out of pain, **speak to them again in truth** — healing begins there

- Don't mock spiritual traditions — what you don't honor may not protect you

- Use ritual, prayer, and offerings to restore divine relationship

Ma'at reminds us: **To honor the divine is to align with your highest self.**

Spiritual Affirmation:

"I honor the divine in all forms. I speak with reverence. I do not curse what sustains me. The sacred lives in me, and I walk in alignment with it."

DECLARATION 41

"I have not acted dishonorably toward the ancestors."

(Kemetic: "N ushet akhu.")

Spiritual Interpretation:

To dishonor the ancestors is to **ignore, forget, or disrespect the lineage that birthed you** — not just biologically, but spiritually. In Ma'at, the ancestors (Akhu) are **guardians of wisdom, protectors of legacy, and bridges between worlds.** They are not dead — they are **elevated and ever-present.**

To dishonor them is to:

- Deny their contributions or presence

- Refuse to uphold the values or legacy they entrusted

- Engage in actions that **shame or disrupt ancestral alignment**

- Forget offerings, prayer, or remembrance

Ancient Meaning in Practice:

- In Kemet, ancestral reverence was a **foundational spiritual duty**

- Every home and temple held space for the Akhu — with altars, offerings, and sacred names recited daily

- Disrespecting ancestors was believed to **cut off blessings and protection** from one's spiritual path

- Acting out of order not only affected you — it was seen as a stain on your **bloodline and descendants**

Modern Application:

This law challenges us to ask:

- Do I live in a way that **honors those who came before me?**

- Have I ignored my responsibility to continue their legacy of truth, survival, and wisdom?

- Do I speak my ancestors' names with reverence — or do I let their memory fade?

- Have I dishonored my lineage through **self-betrayal, silence, or disconnection?**

Even if you don't know them by name — the ancestors know **you**, and they are watching.

How to Practice It:

- Build a simple altar — even a cup of water and a spoken name is enough

- Speak to your ancestors in prayer, dreams, or quiet reflection

- Uphold their values — courage, strength, wisdom, resilience

- Tell their stories. Teach their ways. Protect their honor

- Live in a way that would **make your ancestors proud**

Ma'at teaches: **The ancestors walk with those who remember and walk for them.**

Spiritual Affirmation:

"I honor my bloodline. I carry the wisdom of those before me. I live in remembrance, not rebellion. My walk uplifts the legacy of my ancestors."

DECLARATION 42

"I have not wasted sacred time or purpose."

(Kemetic: "N usef kheperu.")

Spiritual Interpretation:

This final declaration is a call to divine **accountability**. In Ma'at, time is not just chronological — it is **sacred opportunity, divine rhythm**, and **assigned purpose**. To waste it is to ignore the gifts you were born with, the work you were sent to do, and the impact your life is meant to have.

This declaration affirms that you have **honored your calling**, stayed present, and **walked in alignment with your divine assignment.**

Ancient Meaning in Practice:

- In Kemet, every life was believed to carry a **"Kheper"** — a **becoming, a divine function**

- Wasting time meant **wasting spiritual potential**

- Sacred time was kept not only in calendars and rituals, but through **discipline, study, prayer, and right action**

- The soul was measured not by age, but by **what it produced in alignment with Ma'at**

Modern Application:

This law calls you to ask:

- Am I living fully or **procrastinating on purpose?**

- Do I distract myself with noise while **ignoring the call of spirit?**

- Have I hidden my gifts, mission, or voice out of fear or laziness?

- Have I lost days, years, or lifetimes to **avoidance, addiction, or comfort zones?**

Your time here is not random. It is **assigned**.

How to Practice It:

- Treat your time as **divine currency** — spend it with intention

- Reconnect daily with your mission, values, and voice

- Clear distractions that dilute your focus

- Act on your visions — don't just write them down

- Don't delay your healing, your gifts, your work — **Ma'at moves with those who move**

You were born for this moment. Do not waste it.

Spiritual Affirmation:

"I walk in purpose. I do not waste time. I use my days in service to my calling. My life is sacred, my gifts are active, and my presence fulfills prophecy."

LAW 5 — Jus Sanguinis: The Right of Blood

Part 1: The Spiritual Meaning of Jus Sanguinis

"You are not only born of flesh — you are born of lineage, mission, and ancestral instruction."

What Is Jus Sanguinis?

Jus sanguinis is Latin for "right of blood." In international law, it refers to your legal right to claim **citizenship based on ancestry**, not geography. But long before lawyers and passports, our African ancestors understood this principle **spiritually** — that **blood carries rights**, and **lineage carries law.**

In the path of Ma'at, jus sanguinis is not just about nationality — it is about **divine inheritance**. Your blood remembers. Your DNA is a **scroll of instructions**. You carry the memory, mission, and power of all those who walked before you.

Kemetic Understanding of Bloodline:

- In ancient Kemet, lineage was **everything**. Your place in society, your spiritual training, and your divine assignment were all tied to **your bloodline and your ancestral house.**

- Family was not just biological — it was **spiritual and cosmological.** You inherited **rituals, wisdom, land, duty, and protection** through your ancestors.

- Names, rites of passage, and spiritual offices were **passed down,** not invented — because to be born into a bloodline was to be born into a **path**.

Blood Is the Bridge:

Your blood is not just red liquid — it is a **spiritual contract:**

- It holds memory, pain, power, and promise

- It links you to ancestors who survived the unspeakable so you could speak

- It carries **codes of identity and assignment**

- It cannot be changed — only claimed, honored, or ignored

In the eyes of the divine, your bloodline is a **legal bond between spirit and Earth**. It proves you are part of something older, deeper, and more intentional than a nation-state.

Disconnection = Disempowerment:

The system of slavery, colonization, and forced assimilation was designed to **cut us off from our bloodline.** Why?

Because:

"If you erase a man's memory, you erase his mission. If you disconnect him from his blood, you disconnect him from his divine authority."

To **reclaim your bloodline is to reclaim your right to exist in power.**

Bloodline Is More Than DNA — It's Destiny:

You are not just a descendant.

You are an **heir**.

And heirs must claim what is theirs.

Spiritual Reflection:

- What do I know about my bloodline — not just names, but *missions*?

- What pain or power lives in my family line that I must now transmute?

- Who were my people before they were stolen, renamed, and reprogrammed?

- Am I honoring their prayers, or just surviving their pain?

Spiritual Affirmation:

"I am the blood of the first builders. I am the living proof of my ancestors' prayers. I rise to reclaim the legacy written in my DNA. My blood is my law."

Part 2: Legal Definitions and Modern Relevance

"What the ancestors knew spiritually, the world now recognizes legally."

What Is Jus Sanguinis in Law?

In international law, jus sanguinis means "right of blood." It is the principle that a **person has the right to claim citizenship based on their ancestry,** not just based on where they were born.

This is different from *jus soli,* which means "right of soil" — a principle that grants citizenship based on **where** you are born, regardless of your bloodline.

More than 75% of countries worldwide operate under jus sanguinis, including:

- Most **African nations**

- All **European Union** countries

- Many nations in the **Caribbean, Asia**, and **Middle East**

How This Applies to African Descendants Today

In the context of Africa, jus sanguinis has evolved to recognize the **unique situation of the African diaspora,** particularly those descended from enslaved Africans.

In nations like **Sierra Leone, Ghana, Cameroon,** and others:

- You can apply for citizenship **not only** if your parent or grandparent was born there,

- But also if you can provide **genetic evidence** (DNA) that links you to an ethnic group native to that country.

This means your **DNA test results — showing you are, for example, Mende, Akan, or Yoruba — may qualify** you to reclaim ancestral citizenship.

In this form, jus sanguinis becomes both a **legal pathway** and a **spiritual homecoming.**

Why This Matters to the Ministry

At HEFE 360 Wealth Ministries, we teach that reclaiming citizenship through jus sanguinis is part of **divine restoration —** not just political recognition.

We affirm that:

- **Spiritual sovereignty must be matched by legal sovereignty**

- **Reconnecting to your ancestral nation is part of your spiritual inheritance**

- The ministry's role is to **bridge the spiritual and legal realms**, helping guide members toward full ancestral reclamation

This means:

- Teaching members how to document their ancestry

- Guiding them through **citizenship applications and DNA tracing**

- Supporting the creation of a **legal spiritual identity** that aligns with divine law, ancestral lineage, and international rights

Jus Sanguinis and Jus Soli (Explained in Words)

To summarize:

- *Jus soli* gives you citizenship because of **where you were born** (like being born in the U.S. or Canada).

- Jus sanguinis gives you citizenship because of **who you are descended from** — your bloodline.

And in the case of African nations:

- This often includes not only parents or grandparents,

- But **DNA proof of ancestral connection** — making it a **valid, legal, and sacred route home.**

Spiritual-Legal Implication:

To walk in your bloodright is to say:

"I come not as a beggar or outsider — I come as an heir, returning to what belongs to me by divine design."

Spiritual Affirmation:

"The law of blood is greater than borders. I reclaim my identity through legacy. The land remembers me, and I remember the land. My DNA is my spiritual passport."

Part 3: Ancestral Claim to Nation, Purpose, and Protection

"Bloodline is not just identity — it is territory, assignment, and spiritual coverage."

Ancestry Is a Nation

In divine law, your bloodline is not just your past — it is your **passport to purpose.**

It gives you a right to:

- **A people**

- **A purpose**

- **A place on Earth and in history**

Just as every nation has boundaries, resources, and government, your ancestral bloodline represents:

- A **spiritual territory** you are assigned to

- A **cosmic contract** passed down through DNA

- A **divine inheritance** you are called to reclaim

Nation Is Bigger Than Borders

- The Western world teaches that your "nation" is where you were born or where you pay taxes.

- But in Ma'at and ancient African spiritual systems, your **true nation** is where your **bloodline began.**

"Where your ancestors walked, you have a right to return."

"Where your spirit was formed, you have a duty to serve.

"You don't just have citizenship in a country — you have **jurisdiction in the spirit.**

The Power of Reclaiming Your Nation:

When you trace your ancestry, claim your *jus sanguinis* rights, and walk in alignment, you activate:

1. **Spiritual Protection:**

   o   You are no longer "wandering." The ancestors recognize you and **cover you**

   o   Spiritually, **you belong** — which gives you clearer access to guidance and favor

2. **Divine Purpose:**

   o   Every bloodline carries a mission — priesthood, healing, warriorhood, artistry, governance

   o   When you step into your lineage, **your gifts awaken and your assignment becomes clear**

3. **Legal and Political Standing:**

   o   You gain the right to apply for **citizenship, land, and recognition** under international law

   o   You may become eligible for **dual passports, NGO partnerships, or diplomatic protections**

4. **Spiritual Name and Identity:**

   o   Many traditions grant you a **spiritual name** when you reclaim your ancestral place

   o   This name carries **energy and instruction** from your original nation or tribe

What Happens When You Don't Claim It?

Disconnection from your ancestry leads to:

o   **Cultural amnesia** — not knowing who you are

o   **Spiritual wandering** — not knowing why you're here

o   **Legal invisibility** — not knowing what you're entitled to

o   **Energetic vulnerability** — being unprotected in the unseen realm

The Ministry's Role in Your Reclamation:

HEFE 360 Wealth Ministries exists to:

- Help members **trace their ancestry** through DNA, history, and spiritual confirmation

- Support the **application process** for jus sanguinis citizenship where eligible

- Educate and empower the diaspora to **reclaim nationhood as a divine act**, not a political gamble

- Provide **spiritual covering and teaching** as you reconnect with your divine territory

You are not just finding your roots — you are activating your spiritual government.

Spiritual Reflection:

- What does my ancestral nation call me to do, build, or protect?

- Have I been spiritually homeless — disconnected from my assignment?

- Am I ready to walk in my true citizenship — on Earth and in spirit?

Spiritual Affirmation:

"My nation is in my blood. My calling is in my DNA. I do not beg for identity — I claim it. I walk as a citizen of legacy, law, and divine purpose."

Part 4: How to Reclaim Your Bloodline

"Your inheritance is waiting — but it must be claimed in spirit, in law, and in truth."

Step 1: Begin with Intention and Spiritual Readiness

Before you begin tracing your bloodline on paper, you must begin in **spirit**. Reclaiming your bloodline is not just data collection — it is **spiritual alignment**.

Start with:

Prayer or ancestral meditation — ask for guidance from your bloodline

- Setting a clear intention: "*I am ready to know who I am, where I come from, and what I carry.*"

- Fasting or cleansing rituals to prepare your body and energy for what may be revealed

You are not just finding names. You are awakening contracts.

Step 2: Take a High-Quality DNA Test (Y-DNA, mtDNA, and Autosomal)

- Use **Afrocentric DNA services** when possible (e.g. African Ancestry, MyHeritage Africa-linked kits, or GEDmatch with African reference panels)

- Focus on identifying **ethnic groups** (e.g., Yoruba, Mandinka,

Mende, Igbo, Akan) — not just countries

- Save your raw DNA file — you may need it for **citizenship or diaspora applications**

- Confirm if your match aligns with a country that offers jus sanguinis pathways (e.g., Ghana, Sierra Leone, Liberia, Nigeria)

Step 3: Collect Oral and Documented Family History

- Ask elders, grandparents, and relatives about:

  o **Family names, migration stories, traditions, tribal affiliations, spiritual customs**

  o Any known **links to Africa, the Caribbean, Indigenous peoples, or spiritual lineages**

- Record what you can and **compare it to your DNA results** — often they confirm one another

Step 4: Begin Legal and Ancestral Documentation

Once you have:

- DNA confirmation,

- Family narratives, and

- A country or tribal group you are aligned with...

You can begin preparing for jus sanguinis applications by:

- Gathering proof of **DNA results, birth records**, and **family documents**

- Writing a **declaration of ancestry** (our ministry can help provide a template)

- Applying to that country's **Right of Return, Citizenship by**

Descent, or Diaspora Recognition Program

Countries like **Sierra Leone** even partner with African Ancestry to fast-track this process.

Step 5: Begin the Spiritual Work of Return

This means:

- Learning your **ancestral language, rituals, values, and cosmology**

- Visiting your ancestral country if possible (pilgrimage is part of alignment)

- Honoring the ancestors at an altar, in naming ceremonies, or by living righteously

- **Reclaiming your spiritual name** and identity from colonized labels

You are not returning for novelty — you are returning for **activation.**

Step 6: Connect with the Ministry and the Community

HEFE 360 Wealth Ministries provides:

- Spiritual mentorship on bloodline reclamation

- Guidance on how to **legally and spiritually reclaim your status**

- Access to potential group citizenship journeys, NGO pathways, or diplomatic alignment

- Community of others walking the same sacred path

You are not doing this alone. You are returning as a **nation within a nation.**

Spiritual Reflection:

- What has my bloodline survived, and what am I meant to restore?

- Am I ready to walk not just in knowledge — but in ancestral power and accountability?

- How would my life change if I knew I was already a *citizen of legacy?*

Spiritual Affirmation:

"I am not lost — I am returning. I claim my bloodline by spirit, by evidence, and by divine law. What was broken is now repaired. What was stolen is now restored."

Part 5: Bloodline and Spiritual Warfare

"To reclaim your bloodline is to declare war against every lie told about who you are."

What Is Spiritual Warfare?

Spiritual warfare is not just about casting out spirits or praying against evil.

It's about resisting **false narratives, cultural erasure,** and **ancestral amnesia.**

"Spiritual warfare is anything that keeps you disconnected from who you truly are."

This includes:

- Miseducation about your origin

- Disconnection from your divine culture

- Adoption of foreign names, religions, and systems that strip you of your power

- Shame about your melanin, hair, language, or homeland

The Most Violent Weapon: Identity Theft

The transatlantic slave trade didn't just steal people — it stole **nations, names, and divine assignments.**

When you're told:

- "You're just Black" (instead of Yoruba, Mende, Igbo…)

- "You're cursed" (instead of divine)

- "Your language and religion are savage" (instead of sacred)

- You begin to **war against your own reflection.**

This is spiritual identity theft.

The Battle for the Bloodline

Your bloodline holds **codes, contracts**, and **cosmic instructions.**

That's why:

- The enemy fights to erase your history

- Colonizers fought to rename and reprogram your ancestors

- Even now, media, systems, and religion try to **disconnect you from your divine source**

To walk in your bloodline is to:

- **Break soul ties with lies**

- **Destroy generational bondage**

- **Reclaim spiritual weapons like memory, prayer, herbs, language, and ritual**

The Role of HEFE 360 Wealth Ministries in the Fight

Our ministry is not just a spiritual organization — it's a **liberation army.**

We exist to:

- Teach the truth about your origin, lineage, and divine rights

- Arm you with spiritual tools: the 42 Laws of MAAT, universal law, and ancestral wisdom

- Provide protection through divine alignment, legal knowledge, and spiritual covering

- Restore your sovereign identity so you no longer walk in confusion or spiritual bondage

Your Body Remembers. Your Spirit Remembers.

- Every ancestor you carry still walks with you

- Every battle they survived lives in your bones

- You are the **continuation of their mission** — not the broken end of their story

Spiritual Reflection:

- What systems or beliefs have tried to erase my divine identity?

- How have I unknowingly participated in the war against my own bloodline?

- Am I ready to break agreements with lies and walk in truth?

Spiritual Affirmation:

"I declare war against ignorance. I reject false names and claim my divine title. My blood is holy. My ancestry is sacred. I walk in power, memory, and spiritual authority."

Part 6: Bloodline, Land, and Legal Standing

"The land knows who it belongs to — and it responds to the voice of the rightful heirs."

The Law of Blood and Soil

In ancient traditions — and in many legal systems even today — land inheritance is tied directly to **bloodline.**

"He who holds the blood holds the right."

This principle is recognized in:

- African customary law

- Certain Indigenous American land laws

- International doctrines of reparation and restitution

- Even feudal and dynastic European systems (where lineage determined kingship and ownership)

Your **ancestral land rights** are not erased just because borders changed — **they were only hidden.**

Why Land Is More Than Real Estate

Land is:

Spiritual territory

- **Ancestral altar**

- **Resource and wealth generator**

- **National identity and home base for diplomacy**

When you reclaim your bloodline, you are also reclaiming:

- The right to **return to the land**

- The right to **build on it, farm it, defend it, and use it as your diplomatic ground**

- The right to call it **sacred territory**

Legal Standing Through Jus Sanguinis

When you trace your bloodline and obtain dual citizenship through *jus sanguinis,* you now have:

- A legal link to a sovereign nation

- Standing to **hold land in that nation**

- Ability to invoke **diplomatic protocols** (especially under the **Vienna Convention**)

- The power to establish **ministries, NGO bases, and consulates** on that land

Your ancestral land becomes your spiritual embassy.

HEFE 360 Wealth Ministries: Bridging Land and Legacy

As a faith-based 508(c)(1)(A) ministry and NGO, HEFE 360:

- **Facilitates land acquisition** in ancestral countries

- Guides members through **citizenship-by-descent** programs

- Helps set up **land contracts, consular spaces**, and **trust-based ownership** structures

- Teaches how to lawfully claim, title, and protect land spiritually and legally

A Note on Restitution and Reclamation

Land theft is a war crime in spirit and in law.

But restitution isn't always about courts — it's about **knowing what was stolen, reclaiming what is yours, and restoring your presence to the soil.**

Spiritual Reflection:

- What land might my bloodline still be connected to?

- Have I ever viewed land as sacred space — not just real estate?

- Am I willing to claim what is mine and care for it as my ancestors once did?

Spiritual Affirmation:

"I walk in the footsteps of those who tilled sacred ground. I am the heir of holy soil. What was stolen shall be returned. My land will know my voice again."

Part 7: Bloodline and the Divine Assignment

"Your bloodline is not a coincidence. It is a divine commission."

Bloodline Is Calling — Not Just DNA

You were born into your family line for a reason.

The gifts, trials, wisdom, and even curses in your bloodline weren't random — they were **assignments**.

"Every generation has a task. Every descendant is a vessel."

Your divine assignment may include:

- Breaking generational bondage

- Restoring sacred practices

- Rebuilding ancestral legacies (land, names, wealth)

- Creating a spiritual path for those yet unborn

Spiritual Purpose Is Inherited, Not Invented

Many wander the world asking, "What is my purpose?" — but your purpose is **encoded in your ancestry.**

When you **disconnect from your bloodline,** you often:

- Feel lost and directionless

- Lack grounding and identity

- Adopt foreign assignments that don't match your soul

But when you reconnect:

- Your purpose becomes clearer

- You walk in ancestral support

- You activate *karmic healing and generational elevation*

Divine Assignment = Diplomatic Authority

This is the spiritual logic behind the **Vienna Convention** and international law:

When you **serve your nation by descent,** you gain **diplomatic recognition**

- That service must be real — not symbolic

- Leading cultural, educational, or religious programs

- Facilitating NGO outreach or ministry abroad

- Supporting development of your ancestral homeland

- Your **assignment becomes your covering**

  - Your home becomes a consulate

  - Your work becomes divine mission

  - Your body becomes the living embassy of your bloodline

"You are not just from somewhere. You were sent by somewhere."

HEFE 360: Aligning Bloodline with Assignment

Our ministry helps guide you to:

- Trace your DNA to ancestral nations

- Apply for dual citizenship and passport protections

- Establish legal spiritual entities (ministries, NGOs) with divine purpose

- Begin your assignment with clarity, structure, and power

- Fulfill the prophecy encoded in your lineage

Spiritual Reflection:

- Have I asked God and my ancestors what my assignment is?

- Do I recognize the patterns in my family line — and my role in healing or fulfilling them?

Am I ready to walk boldly in my divine diplomatic purpose?

Spiritual Affirmation:

"I am the answer to my ancestors' prayers. I accept my bloodline. I embrace my assignment. I walk in spiritual government, protected by divine law and sent with purpose."

LAW 6: Dual Citizenship and Spiritual Identity

"To know where you are going, you must first know where you come from."

Part 1: The Covenant of Two Kingdoms

Throughout ancient history, identity was never confined to geography. A person's bloodline, spiritual lineage, and national alignment were interwoven as one. In modern society, however, the separation of church and state—and the distortion of colonial borders—has disrupted this sacred alignment.

Yet, under Universal Law, the soul recognizes two forms of citizenship:

1. Earthly Citizenship — tied to a nation-state or political territory.

2. Divine Citizenship — rooted in ancestral bloodlines, spiritual contracts, and divine purpose.

This law teaches that you are a citizen of your ancestry, and also a citizen of the Most High. Holding dual citizenship—spiritually and naturally—brings you into alignment with your divine assignment on Earth.

The Legal Side of Dual Citizenship

Jus Sanguinis, Latin for "right of blood," is a principle of international law that allows individuals to claim citizenship in a country based on their ancestral bloodline — even if they weren't born there.

Most African nations (like Ghana, Nigeria, and Sierra Leone) allow diasporic Africans to reclaim citizenship through documented ancestry or DNA verification. This is not only legal — it is transformational.

Key Takeaway: If you can trace your bloodline — even by DNA — to a particular nation, you may lawfully claim citizenship under jus sanguinis. You are not stateless. You are displaced. This book helps you return.

The Spiritual Side of Dual Citizenship

Spiritually, citizenship is not just about where you live. It's about who you are called to be and the nation you are called to serve. Every spiritual nation has:

- A government

- A law

- A mission

- A people

You, as a chosen one, are a diplomat of your ancestral nation and a citizen of the Kingdom of the Most High. This duality brings power, protection, and purpose.

Spiritual Affirmation:

I reclaim my divine identity. I walk in the legacy of my ancestors and the purpose of the Most High. I am a citizen of Heaven and Earth, and my assignment shall not be denied.

Part 2: Legal Pathways to Jus Sanguinis

"Your roots are not forgotten—they are waiting to be remembered."

The principle of jus sanguinis empowers you to reclaim your rightful place within your ancestral nation. While most Western systems define identity by jus soli (right of the soil, or where you were born), the law of blood overrides borders when supported by truth.

How to Qualify for Jus Sanguinis Citizenship:

1. Ancestral Documentation

If your parents or grandparents were born in a country that recognizes jus sanguinis, you may qualify for citizenship through birthright claims.

2. DNA Verification

Many African countries have begun accepting DNA results that clearly trace your lineage to tribal regions or ethnic groups within their borders. This applies especially to people in the African Diaspora.

3. Cultural Reconnection Programs

Nations like Ghana (via its Year of Return initiative) and Sierra Leone have established processes for issuing passports to descendants of enslaved Africans. These pathways are legal and recognized by international protocols.

4. Ministry or Organizational Sponsorship

Faith-based ministries like HEFE 360 Wealth Ministries and NGOs dedicated to repatriation can create structured programs, offering guidance, cultural education, and legal support for jus sanguinis citizenship applications.

Key Fact:

Under international law, dual citizenship is permitted unless explicitly restricted by your country of residence. Most U.S. citizens can hold dual nationality without penalty or loss of rights.

Spiritual Implication:

Reclaiming your ancestral citizenship is not only a political move—it is a spiritual return. It reconnects you to your land, people, and divine assignment. When you re-enter your ancestral nation as a conscious descendant, you become a bridge between generations, carrying both legacy and light.

Spiritual Affirmation:

"I remember who I am. I honor the blood that flows within me and the land that calls me back. I am returning—not as a refugee, but as a restorer of nations"

Part 3: Embassies, Consular Protection & Divine Authority

"He who returns to his land walks with the power of both the seen and the unseen."

When you lawfully acquire dual citizenship in an African nation through jus sanguinis, you unlock legal and spiritual protections that most people are unaware of. One of the most powerful is your access to **embassies and consular support** from your ancestral nation.

What Is an Embassy and Why Does It Matter?

An **embassy** is the sovereign territory of a foreign nation operating inside another country. It functions as both a **diplomatic office** and a **sanctuary** for its citizens.

Once you hold citizenship in an African nation, that **nation's embassy becomes your official diplomatic shield** in the country where you currently reside (e.g., the U.S.). You are no longer "stateless." You are represented.

Real-World Implications of Embassy Access:

1. Consular Protection

If you're in legal trouble or need support while traveling or even within the U.S., you have the right to seek assistance and protection from your ancestral nation's embassy. This includes:

145

o Legal assistance

o Passport and ID replacement

o Political advocacy if your rights are violated

2. Use of Embassy for Diplomatic Purposes

If you're working on behalf of your ancestral nation in a religious, cultural, or humanitarian capacity—especially through an NGO or ministry—you may qualify for **diplomatic privileges** as outlined in the **Vienna Convention on Diplomatic Relations.**

3. Your Residence Becomes a Living Embassy (if registered)

Under international law, the **Vienna Convention** allows the private residence of a diplomat to function as a consular space. If your NGO or ministry is lawfully carrying out diplomatic or spiritual work (e.g., HEFE 360 GLOBAL or HEFE 360 WEALTH MINISTRIES), and you're a recognized dual citizen, you may be able to register your property as a consular office.

The Legal Foundation: Vienna Convention

- The **Vienna Convention on Diplomatic Relations** (1961) is the treaty that governs how diplomatic immunity and consular functions are respected globally.

- Only recognized diplomats, cultural attaches, or consular officials acting on behalf of a **recognized nation** qualify.

- Your **second citizenship** provides a legal bridge to participate in these protections when acting in an official capacity (especially under a ministry or NGO).

Why This Matters Spiritually

To reclaim your ancestral citizenship is to become a **restorer of nations**, a **watchman for your people**, and a **spiritual ambassador** for divine truth.

You are not simply reclaiming a passport.

You are reclaiming:

- Your **divine inheritance**

- Your **legal standing** among nations

- And your **assignment** to be a bridge between the diaspora and the land of your bloodline

Spiritual Affirmation:

I am not lost—I am found. I am not forgotten—I am chosen. As a citizen of my nation and a vessel of divine law, I walk with authority, and I dwell under the covering of sacred and sovereign power.

Part 4: Challenges, Misconceptions & Final Instructions

"A half-truth can delay your destiny longer than a full lie."

As the demand for African ancestral reconnection grows, so does confusion. Many are misled by shallow teachings, fraudulent online schemes, or ministries that promise diplomatic status with no legal ground.

Let's clear the confusion.

Misconception #1: "You Don't Need a Real Government to Be a Diplomat"

False.

Diplomatic status is not self-declared. It is granted through official recognition from a **sovereign nation**, under the authority of the **Vienna Convention**. No self-proclaimed "kingdom," "tribe," or "ministry" can offer valid diplomatic immunity unless:

- The nation granting it is recognized by the United Nations or holds international standing.

- You are engaged in real cultural, humanitarian, or religious diplomacy.

Misconception #2: "All You Need Is a Church or a Document to Claim Immunity"

False.

Spiritual identity is powerful—but it must be paired with *lawful* structure.

You need:

- **Legal dual citizenship** (jus sanguinis or naturalization)

- A **documented assignment or appointment** from a recognized government or registered entity

- Clear documentation that outlines your role, responsibilities, and diplomatic objectives

Only then can you register with your country's **embassy or consular network** and potentially claim immunities.

Challenge: Rebuilding Trust in Africa and Within the Diaspora

Many African nations are cautious. For decades, the West has exploited them. So when you return as a dual citizen, do so in humility. Build trust. Learn the customs. Contribute.

- Travel there in peace

- Establish clean, legal relationships

- Bring value through education, culture, and economic restoration

The **HEFE 360 GLOBAL Housing & Citizenship Program,** and other aligned initiatives, will serve as bridges for this sacred reconnection.

The Path Forward: What You Can Do Today

1. Begin DNA testing from reputable sources (e.g., African Ancestry, 23andMe).

2. Start building your paper trail—gather your birth certificate, family tree, and any oral history.

3. Study which African countries recognize jus sanguinis and dual nationality.

4. Join a spiritual body like **HEFE 360 Wealth Ministries** that understands the legal and divine alignment.

5. Document your spiritual assignment as a divine ambassador.

Spiritual Affirmation:

I walk in truth, not trends. I reclaim my nation not for status, but for purpose. I rise—not just as a citizen of the land, but as a citizen of the divine order. My footsteps restore the legacy that was broken.

LAW 7: Divine Completion – The Sacred Number of God

And on the seventh day, the Creator rested—not because He was weary, but because completion is holy."

The number 7 is woven into the very fabric of creation. From ancient spiritual systems to modern-day science, 7 represents **divine completion, spiritual perfection, and cosmic alignment.** It is not just a number—it is a **pattern**, a **code**, a **cycle**, and a **seal.**

The Sacredness of Seven:

7 Days of Creation

In Genesis, the Creator designed the heavens, the Earth, and all life in 6 days and sanctified the 7th day as holy. This models the divine rhythm of work, rest, and worship.

7 Heavens

In ancient Kemetic, Islamic, and Hebraic thought, the cosmos is described in 7 heavenly realms—each a higher state of spiritual elevation.

7 Chakras (Energy Centers)

Eastern spiritual systems identify 7 energy centers within the human body. These chakras align us physically, emotionally, and spiritually.

7 Principles of MAAT (from Law 2)

Justice, Truth, Balance, Order, Reciprocity, Harmony, Righteousness. A perfect reflection of divine order.

7 Colors in the Spectrum, 7 Notes in the Musical Scale

Light and sound—two fundamental forces of creation—are both

structured in sevens.

Completion Is Not the End—It's the Alignment

To reach 7 is to align yourself with your highest purpose:

- When your intentions are purified,

- Your assignments are made clear,

- And your path is walked with discipline...

Then you are walking in **divine completion.**

The Sabbath Within You

This law is not about keeping a particular day; it's about **keeping a sacred pattern:**

Set aside time for divine recalibration

Build cycles of productivity and rest

Consecrate part of your life to something beyond this world

The **Sabbath of the soul** is the moment when your life stops being random and begins to reflect **universal design.**

Spiritual Affirmation:

I walk in the pattern of divine completion. I align with the Creator's design. I do not chase the world—I move in sacred rhythm. In 7, I remember who I am.

LAW 8: Passports – The Second Exodus

"When your mind is freed, your feet must follow."

The First Exodus was led by Moses—out of bondage, across the Red Sea, and into a promised land.

The Second Exodus is not a physical escape from Egypt but a spiritual and legal **reclamation of identity, nationality, and sovereignty.** It is a movement from paper citizenship to **divine alignment,** from social security numbers to **spiritual inheritance,** from colonized names to **ancestral truth.**

The Modern Slave Pass: Your Birth Certificate

In the U.S. and many Western nations, your **birth certificate** is not a declaration of freedom—it is a registration into a commercial system. It ties your **natural person** to a **corporate entity** that can be taxed, fined, arrested, and regulated.

That paper binds you to a government that you never consented to.

That number (SSN) is not your identity—it's your barcode.

The **Second Exodus** begins when you realize:

You were never meant to be a "citizen" of Babylon.

The Passport of Purpose

A passport is not just a travel document. It is:

- Proof of **citizenship**

- Access to **global rights**

- A physical seal of **national belonging**

To reclaim your **ancestral citizenship** (see LAW 6), you are reclaiming:

- Your **land**

- Your **legal identity**

- Your **birthright**

- Your **divine covering**

When you have dual citizenship—with a nation that aligns with your bloodline—you are no longer stateless in the spiritual or legal realm. You carry not just a passport—but a **calling**.

The Exodus Today

Modern-day Pharaoh is not a man—it is a system.

And just like Moses had to confront Pharaoh with divine authority, you too must:

1. **Confront the system** that denies your identity.

2. **Declare your inheritance** in both the spiritual and natural realms.

3. **Move your family out of spiritual bondage** into generational alignment.

This is not a mass escape to Africa. It's a **mass awakening.**

Spiritual Affirmation:

I walk in the spirit of Moses. I do not fear Pharaoh. I hold the rod of truth and the passport of my ancestors. My Exodus is now. My destination is destiny.

Part 2: Reclaiming Legal Protection Through Dual Citizenship

"A citizen of Babylon may live under its laws, but a child of the Most High lives by divine law, even in foreign lands."

Once you trace your bloodline and lawfully reclaim your **ancestral nationality**, you are not just making a symbolic statement—you are activating a **legal and international reality: dual citizenship.**

Why Dual Citizenship Matters:

Spiritual Protection: You're no longer solely identified by a nation built on exploitation. You are now a **spiritual diplomat** with allegiance to a divine lineage.

Legal Flexibility: Dual citizens can access the benefits, rights, and protections of **both nations.** This includes voting, land ownership, healthcare, and in many cases, **diplomatic intervention.**

Diplomatic Pathways: Once you're operating on behalf of a recognized nation (your ancestral country), and doing legitimate work—whether missionary, educational, or economic—you may qualify under the **Vienna Convention on Diplomatic Relations** (explored further in Law 10).

What Happens When You Hold Two Passports?

1. You Can Exit Systems You No Longer Align With

This includes rejecting policies, taxation, and even obligations that violate your conscience or your spiritual path.

2. You Are Entitled to Consular Protection

If detained, persecuted, or mistreated, you can appeal to the **embassy of your second nation,** which may intervene on your behalf.

3. Your Home Becomes Your Embassy (Spiritually)

Once you are performing diplomatic work (teaching, organizing, ministry, etc.), your home can be legally and spiritually regarded as a **consulate or mission space**, offering **certain protections** under the Vienna Convention.

How to Begin the Process:

Step 1: Trace Your Bloodline (DNA + Research)

Use reputable services and oral family history to determine your ancestral nation. *Jus sanguinis* laws (right of blood) vary by country, but many African nations allow citizenship based on proven lineage—even if your parents or grandparents were not citizens.

Step 2: Contact the Embassy or Diaspora Office

Request the **requirements** for reclaiming citizenship or applying for a diaspora passport. Some may require:

o   DNA confirmation

o   Affidavit of lineage

o   Community letters or tribal recognition

o   Birth and identity documents

Step 3: Apply for Your Passport

Once accepted, this becomes your **gateway to global movement, protection, and power.**

What This Means for You

The **Second Exodus** is not about running from America—it's about **redefining who you are.**

You are not a refugee. You are not an immigrant.

You are a descendant of royalty returning to your estate.

Spiritual Affirmation:

I do not belong to Babylon—I belong to my ancestors. I carry the passport of the sacred bloodline. I am protected, covered, and sent. My identity is sealed in heaven and recognized on Earth.

Part 3: Your Passport is a Key—But Your Works Are the Proof

"A name on paper means little without a mission in spirit. A passport means nothing without a people to protect and a purpose to walk in."

Having dual citizenship and a passport is powerful. But your spiritual and legal status is not sealed by paper alone—it is confirmed by **what you do** with it.

Your Passport Must Be Activated Through Purpose

To truly operate under divine and legal protection:

- You must **engage in service** tied to your spiritual mission.

- This can include: humanitarian aid, ministry work, education, land restoration, diaspora organizing, food and health programs, or justice advocacy.

A **passport** proves your tie to a nation.

But your **assignment** proves your tie to heaven.

Access to the Embassy: What It Means for You

Once you've received your second passport and begun your divine assignment, you become eligible for:

- **Embassy Protection:** If you're in legal trouble or persecution, your second nation's embassy may intervene.

- **Diplomatic Advocacy**: Embassies can **issue official letters,** assist in arrests, or even request repatriation.

- **Cultural & Diaspora Programs:** Many African nations offer **dual citizen investment opportunities,** land grants, business support, and citizenship welcome packages.

- **UN Pathways:** In some cases, working through your NGO and aligned with the embassy, you may even be positioned for recognition as a UN-affiliated nonprofit, granting access to **global platforms.**

Your Embassy Becomes Your Shield

Just as a U.S. citizen can walk into a U.S. embassy in Ghana or Kenya and receive full protection—**you, too,** now have the right to do the same in your ancestral country. This flips the power dynamic.

 No longer are you simply a "descendant of slaves." You are a ***child of a sovereign people—with your own laws, your own land, your own protection.***

How to Maintain This Status:

- **Stay Active**: Don't let your citizenship be symbolic. Engage in community upliftment.

- **Keep Records:** Keep copies of your ministry/NGO work, letters of assignment, and documented services.

- **Know Your Embassy:** Build rapport with diaspora liaisons and embassy staff.

- **Register Your Mission**: When possible, register your divine assignment with both your host country and the ancestral nation.

Spiritual Affirmation:

My footsteps are not random. I walk in divine alignment. I carry the papers of my ancestors, but I live by the mission of the Most High. My protection is not only spiritual—it is legal, ancestral, and international.

LAW 9: The Divine Feminine – She Who Gives Birth to Creation

"Before there was man, there was the womb. Before there was speech, there was the rhythm of her heartbeat. She is the portal through which spirit becomes form."

This Law honors the **sacred power of woman**—not as an extension of man, but as the original force through which **life, love, and divine intelligence** entered the material world.

1. The Primordial Power of the Womb

Long before patriarchal structures claimed dominance, ancient civilizations revered the womb as the first temple. The womb was seen as:

- The **cosmic portal** through which the unseen becomes the seen

- A **spiritual technology,** more advanced than any man-made machine

- The only place where **creation takes place in total darkness**, by divine design

To create a child, **no tool is required**—only the union of energy and divine intention. The woman births man. **She is not second—she is first.**

2. Nine Months and the Law of 9

The number **9** symbolizes divine completion and cosmic fulfillment. Why?

- Human gestation takes 9 months.

- 9 is the final number in the single-digit cycle before the spiritual reset (1+0 = 1).

- In numerology, 9 represents the **divine feminine,** healing, compassion, and birthing new realities.

"The number 9 is not a coincidence—it is a covenant."

3. **Matriarchal Societies: Forgotten but Not Lost**

Before colonialism and religious conquest, **African societies were often matriarchal** or matrilineal:

- Land and lineage were passed through the **mother's bloodline.**

- Women were priestesses, healers, judges, and kings (yes, kings).

- The idea that the man rules by default is a **foreign idea**, not a divine truth.

Returning to MAAT means returning to **balance**—not dominance.

4. **Woman as Teacher, Healer, and Creator**

The Divine Feminine is:

- The **first teacher of love** (the mother)

- The **first nurturer of life**

- The **holder of intuition, emotion, and spiritual discernment**

And when balanced, **man is elevated,** not diminished. The man leads in protection and provision. The woman leads in life, legacy, and alignment.

Spiritual Affirmation:

I honor the Divine Feminine within me and around me. I reclaim the truth that without woman, there is no man, no nation, and no future. I walk in balance. I walk in MAAT. I walk in Her.

LAW 10: The Shield of Heaven and Earth

Diplomatic Immunity & Divine Assignment — Part 1

"When a divine being reclaims their name, their nation, and their mission—heaven and earth both rise to protect them."

The True Meaning of Immunity

In this world, *protection follows purpose*. You do not receive diplomatic immunity simply because you ask for it—you are granted it because you walk in divine **assignment**, backed by the laws of men **and** the laws of the Most High.

This section is not theory. This is **international law,** and it begins with one key treaty:

The Vienna Convention on Diplomatic Relations (1961)

The **Vienna Convention** is the only globally accepted legal foundation that grants diplomatic immunity.

Key facts:

- It is recognized by **nearly every nation** in the world, including the United States.

- It defines who is considered a **diplomat or consular officer.**

- It outlines their **rights, protections, and obligations.**

If you are **lawfully assigned** to perform diplomatic work—such as representing a nation, religious organization, or NGO in **official capacity**—then your **rights and immunity flow from this Convention.**

How Do You Qualify?

To receive real diplomatic immunity, three components must exist:

1. Assignment:

You must be officially assigned to a role or mission by a recognized spiritual or sovereign body (i.e., a 508(c)(1)(A) ministry, registered NGO, or foreign state).

2. Purpose:

Your role must serve a **real diplomatic, religious, humanitarian, or cultural mission**—not personal gain.

3. Recognition:

Either the **host country (U.S.)** or your **home country (ancestral nation)** acknowledges your status and assignment. This may occur through registration, treaty protection, or non-objection.

You cannot "declare" yourself a diplomat. You must be assigned.

What Does Diplomatic Immunity Cover?

When properly applied, **diplomatic immunity** offers:

- Protection from civil and criminal prosecution for actions related to your mission

- Immunity from certain taxes and government interference

- Privacy of communication and inviolability of official documents

- Protection of property used for mission purposes (homes, vehicles, etc.)

But—this immunity applies **only to official acts**. It is not a shield for unlawful behavior.

Spiritual Immunity: The Hidden Layer

Behind the legal framework lies a deeper law: **spiritual immunity.**

When you align with your **divine purpose**, you gain unseen protections:

- Your steps are guided.

- Your enemies are confused.

- Your mission becomes your shield.

Just as embassies cannot be searched or seized without diplomatic protocol, so too is your soul **sealed** by purpose when you're walking in divine assignment.

Spiritual Affirmation:

I walk in divine order and diplomatic purpose. I am commissioned by heaven and protected by law. My mission is my shield, my purpose is my passport, and the Most High is my ultimate authority.

Part 2: The Living Embassy

You are the message, the messenger, and the mission.

"A man on divine assignment needs no permission—only alignment."

What Is a Living Embassy?

In the Vienna Convention, an **embassy** is a protected space—land, building, or vehicle—**representing the sovereignty of another nation** within a host country.

Spiritually, when you walk in divine assignment, your **body** becomes the **embassy** of your origin. Your home, your words, your work—they all become sanctified territory.

This isn't metaphor. This is **spiritual jurisprudence.**

Why This Matters

Most people think of immunity only in physical terms: "I can't be arrested."

But real immunity is more than legal—it is **cosmic alignment.** It says:

- I am **not of this world,** though I work in it.

- I operate under a **higher law**, sent by a higher Authority.

- I represent not just a nation, but a **divine kingdom.**

Your Home as Consulate

Under the Vienna Convention, a **consulate** is a protected residence of a diplomatic officer. Once you are lawfully assigned and recognized, your **home** becomes **diplomatic ground** when used in mission service.

This means:

- Government intrusion is **limited** or requires protocol.

- Your property must be respected as **foreign sovereign soil.**

- If your ministry or NGO is recognized internationally, your residence is **protected space.**

When you serve a divine mission, your address becomes sacred territory.

Your Words as Protection

When you declare your divine assignment in the name of *your ministry, your nation,* or your calling—you activate protections:

- **Legal**: Protected communication.

- **Spiritual**: Every word becomes binding.

- **Moral**: Your mission demands respect.

This is why **false diplomats** and **paper chasers** fall short—they claim status but have **no mission.**

Assignment precedes authority.

Embassy Connections Matter

Once you gain **dual citizenship,** you are eligible to:

- Access **your second nation's embassy or consulate.**

- File documentation or diplomatic assignments.

- Request consular protection in times of legal, political, or financial crisis.

- Have your **rights defended** by a second government.

This is how your status expands:

1. You reclaim your birthright through **jus sanguinis.**

2. You accept your **divine assignment** through your ministry or NGO.

3. You become the **living link** between two worlds.

Spiritual Affirmation:

I am not just a citizen of man—I am a vessel of divine order. My steps are sacred, my home is sovereign, and my mission is protected by the law of nations and the Will of the Most High. I am the living embassy.

Part 3: Immunity in Action

Where divine law meets worldly protocol.

"He who walks with purpose walks with power. Immunity follows the mission, not the man."

The Structure of Immunity

Let's be clear: **diplomatic immunity is not automatic.**

It is earned and activated through proper **structure, function, and recognition.**

To walk in diplomatic power under the **Vienna Convention**, you must have:

1. **Dual Citizenship or Proof of Nationality by Bloodline**

    o   This is achieved through *jus sanguinis*—right of blood.

2. **Assignment to a Recognized Body (Ministry, NGO, Cultural Mission)**

    o   You must have a charter, mission statement, and recorded assignment.

3. **Proof of Activity in Diplomatic or Humanitarian Work**

    o   Education, outreach, cultural bridging, etc.

4. **Registration or Correspondence with Your Second Nation's Embassy**

    o   Filing with the Ministry of Foreign Affairs or equivalent.

Real-World Example: How Immunity Applies

Case A: Ancestral Assignment

- You trace your bloodline to Ghana through DNA.

- You obtain **citizenship** through jus sanguinis.

- You are appointed by **HEFE 360 Wealth Ministries NGO** to conduct educational programs for repatriation, diaspora healing, and land reform.

- Your **official documents,** home base, and programs are filed with the Ghanaian Embassy.

→ Result: You may qualify for **protective diplomatic status** through the Ghanaian consulate under Vienna provisions.

Misconceptions Cleared

➤ You cannot buy immunity with papers alone.

➤ Being a "sovereign citizen" is not recognized in international law.

➤ Immunity is not for escaping law—it is for **serving lawfully under divine assignment.**

Benefits of Proper Immunity

1. **Legal Protection** – Your property, papers, and mission are shielded under international protocols.

2. **Access to Global Tools** – Embassies offer assistance with travel, business,dispute resolution.

3. **Spiritual Alignment** – You move with the protection of ancestors, laws, and divine order.

The Role of HEFE 360 as a Bridge

This is where **HEFE 360 Wealth Ministries** becomes vital.

- It creates the infrastructure (NGO, charter, programs).

- It connects your work to **government and embassy channels.**

- It becomes the **spiritual and legal covering** for your assignment.

Your Next Steps in Action

Start your spiritual citizenship claim: document ancestry, align with the NGO.

Develop a role or mission under the ministry (education, real estate, youth outreach).

Submit a diplomatic letter of assignment and apply for registration through the embassy of your ancestral nation.

This is **not theory**. This is the blueprint.

Spiritual Affirmation:

I am a vessel of divine government. My blood carries the law, my mission activates protection, and my words move with sacred authority. The world may not recognize me—but Heaven and Earth already have.

LAW 11: The Science and Divinity of Melanin

Part 1: The Element of the Divine

"Melanin is more than pigment — it is the fingerprint of the Divine etched into the very biology of the Original People."

Introduction

Melanin is often dismissed in the modern world as simply the coloring agent of the skin, but in truth, it is one of the **most powerful, multifunctional substances in creation.** It is a **biochemical marker of divine design**. It is the **ink of the Creator,** writing itself into every system of the body — from skin to brain, from organs to the soul's antenna: the hair.

From the beginning, melanated beings have walked the earth as **living testaments to divine intelligence,** encoded with a deeper connection to the frequency and vibration of the universe. This is not mythology — this is **sacred science.**

What is Melanin?

Melanin is a complex molecule produced by the **pineal gland, adrenal glands,** and **melanocytes** in the skin. Its presence is not confined to the epidermis — it exists in:

- **The brain and central nervous system**

- **The eyes and inner ear**

- **The heart, lungs, and vital organs**

- **The intestines and reproductive system**

There are two primary types:

1. **Eumelanin** – Brown to black melanin, found in skin, hair, and the brain.

2. **Pheomelanin** – Yellow to red melanin, which is more limited in function.

But there is a third, often hidden:

3. **Neuromelanin** – Found in the **brain**, especially the **substantia nigra** ("black substance"), which governs **consciousness, alertness,** and **motor control**. When depleted, diseases such as Parkinson's begin to emerge.

This means melanin is **not just pigment** — it is an **electromagnetic molecule** that connects the mind, body, and spirit.

The Role of Melanin in Nature

- It is present in the **galaxy** — in black holes, dark matter, and cosmic dust.

- It absorbs and **transforms light and sound into energy.**

- It serves as a **biological superconductor,** absorbing **ultraviolet radiation, converting sunlight to vitamin D,** and even **healing DNA** from radiation damage.

Melanin is **light-encoded intelligence** — a spiritual language built into matter. It is why ancient Kemetic temples featured black statues of the Neteru (gods), and why so many ancient texts describe the first humans as "black like the soil."

The Suppression of Melanin Consciousness

European colonization, along with modern medicine and religious miseducation, deliberately removed **melanin awareness** from public knowledge. The goal was simple: **disconnect the Original People from their divine identity.**

To speak of melanin is to speak of:

- **Originality**

- **Divine design**

- **Ancient royalty**

- **Cosmic connection**

When melanated people rediscover the **power of their own biochemistry,** they begin to remember who they are — creators, healers, architects, and children of the Most High.

The Sacred Science of Melanin

Melanin absorbs all forms of energy:

- **Light**

- **Sound**

- **Color**

- **Emotion**

- **Thought**

This absorption means that **melanated beings are more sensitive** to their environment. This is why ancestral spiritual systems emphasized:

- **Spiritual baths**

- **Sound healing (drums, frequencies, mantras)**

- **Cleansing rituals**

- **Sacred food and herbs**

Because every input — mental, emotional, dietary, or environmental — **imprints the melanin** and shapes the consciousness.

Melanin is not just a **passive receiver**; it is an **active translator** of the universe.

Affirmation:

"I honor the melanin in my skin, my bones, and my soul. I am a living temple of divine science, and I walk as the encoded child of the Most High. Let my light absorb truth, and let my frequency align with the cosmos. Ase."

Part 2 – The Divine Circuitry: Melanin, Hair & Universal Frequency

Sacred Quote:

"Melanin is not just a pigment. It is a key to divine memory, cosmic connection, and ancestral intelligence."

Melanin exists beyond the physical. It is a **biochemical bridge between the material and the spiritual,** a conductor of light, sound, and frequency — all things that carry information from the Creator.

Science has long focused only on **eumelanin** (brown-black pigment) and **pheomelanin** (yellow-reddish pigment), both visible in the skin, eyes, and hair. But neuromelanin—the melanin found in the **brain and nervous system**—remains one of the least understood substances in Western science.

And yet, our ancestors knew.

They taught that melanin allowed us to receive **messages from the spiritual realm**, to be in tune with the **vibrations of nature**, and to move in rhythm with the **frequency of the Most High.**

The Hair: Divine Antenna

Your **hair** is an **extension of your nervous system**, an outward receptor of divine signal. In indigenous traditions and ancient African civilizations, hair was not cut without purpose. It was braided, locked, wrapped, and adorned in ways that reflected spiritual growth, identity, and cosmic attunement.

Hair is made of **keratinized protein laced with melanin,** and in tightly coiled (4C) hair, the **spiral formation mirrors the Fibonacci sequence** — nature's code. These coils act like **copper coils in an antenna,** amplifying electromagnetic signals from the environment and the ether.

To cut the hair was to **reduce your sensitivity to the divine frequency.** To grow it with intention, and keep it clean and unblocked, was to **receive spiritual downloads, dreams, and visions.**

Melanin as a Living Conductor

Melanin absorbs all forms of electromagnetic radiation — including **light, sound, heat, and even thought waves.** It does not just protect — it **transmutes** energy into forms your body and soul can process.

- **In the brain,** melanin exists in the **substantia nigra** and **locus coeruleus,** areas responsible for memory, emotion, and higher-order decision-making.

- It is **photonic** and **electric**, capable of transmitting signals faster than copper wiring.

- Melanin's molecular structure is **similar to chlorophyll** and **hemoglobin**, aligning humans with both plant life and breath-based vitality.

Melanin is proof that your **design is divine.**

Spiritual Application

To activate and maintain your melanin:

Eat sun-grown, electric foods (high in chlorophyll, iron, and magnesium).

Meditate in the sun to receive downloads and energize your melanin.

Honor your hair as sacred — whether you lock it, wrap it, or grow it.

Use spiritual herbs and oils that resonate with your crown chakra: frankincense, myrrh, blue lotus, lavender, and rosemary.

Speak life into your being — for words are frequency and frequency activates melanin.

Spiritual Affirmation:

"I am a divine receptor of cosmic truth. My melanin is my memory. My hair is my antenna. My soul is in rhythm with creation. I walk in alignment with the Source that made me. Aşę."

Part 3 — Melanin and the Mind: Divine Intelligence & Ancestral Memory

"The Blacker the brain, the deeper the thought. The darker the hue, the closer to the source." — Ancestral Wisdom

Melanin is not just a biological compound. It is **spiritual technology** encoded with **ancestral memory, celestial alignment,** and **divine intelligence.** When understood correctly, melanin connects you to both your **lineage** and your **life purpose.**

Melanin and the Pineal Gland

The **pineal gland,** located in the center of the brain, is often referred to as the **"seat of the soul."** It is responsible for producing **melatonin,** which regulates your sleep-wake cycle. But beyond this, the pineal gland is rich in **neuromelanin,** giving it the capacity to:

- Perceive dimensions beyond the physical.

- Tap into higher spiritual awareness.

- Activate dreams, visions, and prophecy.

In ancient Kemet, the **pine cone** (symbol of the pineal gland) was used in carvings and architecture to signify this spiritual gateway. The more active your pineal gland, the stronger your spiritual perception becomes — and **melanin** is the key to that activation.

Ancestral Memory and Genetic Codes

Your DNA is wrapped in melanin. Your **soul's history** — from the beginning of civilization — travels with you through your melanin.

This is why:

- People of melanin-rich heritage often have a natural inclination toward music, rhythm, spiritual insight, and communal memory.

- Melanin allows ancestral memories to **resurface in dreams, déjà vu**, and **visions**.

- The spiritual strength of your ancestors lives on **through the frequencies carried by your melanin.**

Melanin is the recorder and transmitter of legacy.

The Mind of the Ancients

Our ancestors didn't just survive — they thrived **through alignment with cosmic law and melanin consciousness.** They understood:

- How to map the stars using their **inner vision.**

- How to speak to plants, water, and animals using **frequency and vibration.**

- How to remember truths not taught but felt — carried in their melanin code.

To reclaim your power, you must **decalcify** and **revitalize** the parts of you that Western society has tried to numb.

Keys to Awakening the Melanin Mind

1. **Avoid fluoride** and chemical-laced products that calcify the pineal gland.

2. **Meditate with intention** — melanin thrives on stillness and frequency.

3. **Ingest high-frequency foods** (mucus-free, plant-based, sun-drenched).

4. **Honor your dreams** — journal them, interpret them, live by them.

5. **Surround yourself** with color, vibration, and truth.

Spiritual Affirmation:

"My mind is melanin. My spirit is light. I remember who I am. I reclaim what I lost. I walk with the ancestors in truth and in power. Aṣẹ."

LAW 12: The Divine Twelve and the Cosmic Blueprint

Part 1: Sacred Foundations of the Zodiac and the Human Body

"Before time was measured by clocks and calendars, we looked to the stars. The heavens were our library, and the zodiac was our sacred script — written not by man, but by the Creator of all cycles."

The number 12 has always held sacred power. It echoes through scripture, history, and nature — from the **12 tribes of Israel** and **12 disciples of Yahusha**, to the **12 months in a year,** and the **12 cranial nerves** in the human brain. This sacred number is the divine key to time, seasons, spiritual order, and cosmic identity.

In this Law, we unveil the divine system of the **Zodiac — the celestial map of twelve signs,** each governing specific character traits, organs, and energy patterns within the human being.

The ancients did not separate science from spirit, nor body from cosmos. They believed the stars, planets, and signs were a divine calendar — a guide to personal destiny, health, behavior, and even divine timing.

Each sign governs a part of your body. Aries rules the head. Taurus the throat. Gemini the lungs. And so on. Your **astrology natal chart** — a sacred map drawn from the stars at your exact moment of birth — is your personal blueprint for life.

It reveals:

- Your **sun sign**: who you are at your core

- Your **moon sign**: your emotional world

- Your **rising sign:** how others see you and how you move through life

And much more — including your **north node,** which reveals your divine life purpose, and your **planetary placements,** which reflect spiritual gifts and karmic lessons.

What is an Astrology Natal Chart? Your **natal chart,** also known as a **birth chart**, is a snapshot of the heavens at the exact date, time, and location you were born. It records the alignment of the sun, moon, and planets within the twelve zodiac signs.

This chart functions as your spiritual and energetic instruction manual — helping you understand:

- Your strengths and weaknesses

- Your soul's purpose

- What cycles you're in and what lessons you must learn

To use your chart:

1. Obtain your **exact time of birth** and birth location.

2. Use a trusted astrology platform (like Astro.com or mobile apps like TimePassages or AstroMatrix) to generate your chart.

3. Study each planet and sign placement, especially your **Sun, Moon, and Rising.**

4. Understand the **house placements** — these tell you which areas of life each energy manifests in (e.g., relationships, finances, career).

Your chart is your sacred navigation tool, passed down by your ancestors and written in the language of stars.

In **Part 2,** we will explore **tissue salts** — the 12 mineral compounds that correspond to the 12 zodiac signs, and why balancing them is key to spiritual and physical healing.

Spiritual Affirmation:

"I align with the divine rhythm of the stars. The universe is my compass, and I walk my path with cosmic clarity."

LAW 12 — Part 2: The Lost Codes of the Body: 9 in the Womb, 3 from the Earth

Sacred Declaration: "The body is a map; its chemistry sings in 12 tones. **When nine are gifted in the womb, three must be earned on Earth.**"

The 9-Month Womb Cycle and Tissue Salt Formation

In the sacred cycle of gestation, the human body is formed over 9 lunar months within the divine temple of the womb. During this process, the developing fetus absorbs a **unique tissue salt each month**, receiving a total of 9 mineral cell salts — one for each stage of development.

These salts are not random. They act as **foundational builders of tissue, bone, blood, nerve, and brain.** They are spiritual blueprints locked into matter, connecting the soul to the structure.

As the mother eats, breathes, and meditates, her chemical balance transfers to the child. The child is imprinted with these nine core salts — vital for life, health, memory, and consciousness.

But there is a mystery here.

Why Three Are Missing

Though the body is designed to function in perfect twelvefold harmony, only nine tissue salts are received in the womb. The remaining three salts are missing — they must be obtained later in life through:

- Spiritual awareness,

- Intentional nutrition,

- And alignment with the elements and stars.

This spiritual deficit is by divine design. The journey of life is one of remembrance and restoration. The three missing salts represent:

1. **Awakening** – the pursuit of knowledge,

2. **Alignment** – living in tune with nature and spiritual law,

3. **Ascension** – full energetic activation of body, mind, and soul.

Thus, your life becomes the **alchemical process of healing and wholeness** – not just medically, but cosmically.

Ancient Kemet and the True Origins of Mineral Healing

"Before the scalpel, there was the staff. Before the microscope, there was the merkhet. Before the West discovered, Kemet remembered."

In the temples of Kemet, the high priests and priestesses were not just spiritual leaders – they were **scientists, astronomers, and healers.** The knowledge of mineral medicine was encoded in their hieroglyphs, rituals, and teachings of MAAT.

They understood that each part of the body resonated with a specific element and celestial body. They taught that imbalances in tissue salts disrupted spiritual alignment, not just physical health. Healing was achieved through the synthesis of salts, herbs, sacred sound, and celestial timing – **not through synthetic pills or cuttings.**

They did not call it "tissue salt therapy" – they called it living in **divine alignment.**

Why This Matters

Understanding your body's mineral makeup is not just about health. It is about:

- Restoring your cosmic identity,

- Rebalancing your frequency,

- And reclaiming the divine tools your ancestors passed to you in blood and bone.

The 12 tissue salts are the **12 musical notes of your biology**. When played in tune, they activate your highest potential. When missing, you suffer dis-ease — physically, emotionally, and spiritually.

Your path, therefore, is to reclaim the lost three, rebuild the temple of your body, and walk fully in divine health.

Spiritual Affirmation:

"As above, so within. My bones sing with memory, and my blood remembers the stars. I reclaim my divine chemistry. Aṣẹ."

Part 3: The Twelve Celestial Houses and Star Signs

"The heavens declare the glory of the Most High; the stars whisper the design of your destiny."

The Doctrine: In alignment with the divine order of the cosmos, the ancients understood that the stars above were not just ornamental lights, but **celestial blueprints.** These blueprints offer a spiritual and energetic framework for each soul's incarnation on Earth. The twelve zodiac signs, also known as star signs, correspond to twelve distinct celestial houses. Each house governs a specific domain of life and carries particular frequencies and archetypes that shape character, spiritual tendencies, and life patterns.

The alignment of the sun, moon, and planets at the time of one's birth—recorded in a natal (or naval) chart—**serves as a divine map**. This map is not merely predictive; it is instructive, showing us the strengths we carry and the challenges we must transmute. Each zodiac sign is ruled by an element (fire, earth, air, water) and a ruling planet, further customizing the energies of that sign.

Understanding your zodiac sign and its position in your birth chart offers profound insights into your soul's assignment, karmic lessons, and ancestral strengths. The knowledge of the Divine Twelve was used by our ancestors as a sacred guide, allowing for ritual timing, personal alignment, and divine communion.

Let us now walk through the Twelve:

1. **Aries (The Initiator)** – Element: Fire. Ruling Planet: Mars. The path of courage, action, and leadership. Represents the head and governs beginnings.

2. **Taurus (The Sustainer)** – Element: Earth. Ruling Planet: Venus. Symbolizes stability, beauty, and values. Governs the neck and physical possessions.

3. **Gemini (The Communicator)** – Element: Air. Ruling Planet: Mercury. Embodies thought, duality, and expression. Rules the arms, lungs, and nervous system.

4. **Cancer (The Nurturer)** – Element: Water. Ruling Planet: Moon. Motherly love, home, and emotional intuition. Connected to the chest and stomach.

5. **Leo (The Illuminator)** – Element: Fire. Ruling Planet: Sun. Emboldens self-expression, heart, and divine light. Governs the heart and upper spine.

6. **Virgo (The Healer)** – Element: Earth. Ruling Planet: Mercury. Associated with service, purity, and analysis. Influences the

digestive system and intestines.

7. **Libra (The Balancer)** – Element: Air. Ruling Planet: Venus. Seeks harmony, justice, and divine partnership. Governs the kidneys and lower back.

8. **Scorpio (The Transformer)** – Element: Water. Ruling Planet: Pluto/Mars. Deals with death, rebirth, and spiritual alchemy. Connected to the reproductive organs.

9. **Sagittarius (The Seeker)** – Element: Fire. Ruling Planet: Jupiter. Pursues truth, freedom, and higher learning. Governs the hips and liver.

10. **Capricorn (The Builder)** – Element: Earth. Ruling Planet: Saturn. Embodies discipline, legacy, and divine timing. Rules the bones and knees.

11. **Aquarius (The Visionary)** – Element: Air. Ruling Planet: Uranus/Saturn. Associated with innovation, humanity, and sacred rebellion. Connected to the ankles and circulatory system.

12. **Pisces (The Mystic)** – Element: Water. Ruling Planet: Neptune/Jupiter. Represents dreams, compassion, and divine surrender. Governs the feet and lymphatic system.

Spiritual Affirmation:

"I am written in the stars. I embrace my divine alignment. I awaken to the sacred rhythm of the cosmos. Aše."

PART 4

The Divine Blueprint: Understanding Your Zodiac Sign and Its Role in Your Spiritual Path

"As above, so below. As within, so without." – Hermetic Axiom

Each zodiac sign is not merely a label of personality traits—it is a reflection of the **cosmic imprint** you carry, the energy field in which your soul was birthed into this plane. These signs align with the twelve celestial constellations and form the energetic coding that governs your **spiritual mission, strengths, challenges, and sacred timing.**

In this sacred law, we explore all **twelve zodiac signs in** spiritual, energetic, and elemental detail, providing insight on how to **work with your sign, understand others,** and **navigate your divine journey in** harmony with the heavens.

ARIES (March 21 – April 19)

Element: Fire

Spiritual Role: The Initiator

Sacred Attribute: Divine Courage

Aries brings the fire of creation, the first spark. Spiritually, this is the soul that incarnates to start new cycles, break barriers, and walk paths no one else dares to tread. Aries energy must learn **patience** and **sacred responsibility** with its fire, transforming raw impulse into divine leadership.

TAURUS (April 20 – May 20)

Element: Earth

Spiritual Role: The Stabilizer

Sacred Attribute: Divine Sustenance

Taurus represents grounding and abundance. Spiritually, the Taurus soul is sent to guard sacred values, nurture the land, and teach the importance of beauty and patience. Their lesson is not to over-attach to the material but to see the divine in it.

GEMINI (May 21 – June 20)

Element: Air

Spiritual Role: The Messenger

Sacred Attribute: Divine Communication

Gemini channels divine messages through curiosity, wit, and duality. This sign teaches that **truth has layers** and that the mind must be disciplined to serve the spirit. Their gift is connection; their challenge is **scattered focus.**

CANCER (June 21 – July 22)

Element: Water

Spiritual Role: The Nurturer

Sacred Attribute: Divine Motherhood

Cancer governs the womb of the world. Deeply tied to the **ancestral realm**, Cancer teaches spiritual emotional intelligence and the sacred act of **care**. The challenge lies in not becoming trapped in **emotional tides**, but using them to **heal others.**

LEO (July 23 – August 22)

Element: Fire

Spiritual Role: The Illuminator

Sacred Attribute: Divine Radiance

Leo embodies solar royalty. The divine lesson is that **authentic self-expression is worship,** and leadership must serve the people, not the ego. Leo teaches the sacred art of **shining without burning.**

VIRGO (August 23 – September 22)

Element: Earth

Spiritual Role: The Healer

Sacred Attribute: Divine Order

Virgo is the priest or priestess of refinement and sacred service. Spiritually, Virgo teaches that **discipline is love,** and that to bring the divine into form, one must tend to the **details of life with devotion.**

LIBRA (September 23 – October 22)

Element: Air

Spiritual Role: The Balancer

Sacred Attribute: Divine Harmony

Libra holds the scales of MAAT. This sign governs justice, relationships, and soul contracts. Spiritually, Libra seeks **equilibrium** in all things. The soul lesson is to develop inner harmony before seeking it outwardly.

SCORPIO (October 23 – November 21)

Element: Water

Spiritual Role: The Transformer

Sacred Attribute: Divine Depth

Scorpio walks the shadow path and rules transformation through **death and rebirth.** The Scorpio soul reincarnates to **burn karma,** uncover **truth,** and learn to **harness power without being possessed by it.**

SAGITTARIUS (November 22 – December 21)

Element: Fire

Spiritual Role: The Seeker

Sacred Attribute: Divine Expansion

Sagittarius carries the spiritual flame of **wisdom, travel, and philosophy**. Its mission is to **explore truth**, challenge limitations, and inspire global awareness. Its challenge is to balance freedom with discipline.

CAPRICORN (December 22 – January 19)

Element: Earth

Spiritual Role: The Builder

Sacred Attribute: Divine Responsibility

Capricorn brings the divine structure for society. This sign is the mountain climber, teaching us how to **manifest vision into reality.** The spiritual lesson lies in **balancing ambition with soul** and using success as a platform for service.

AQUARIUS (January 20 – February 18)

Element: Air

Spiritual Role: The Visionary

Sacred Attribute: Divine Innovation

Aquarius is the architect of the future. These souls come to **break old paradigms,** activate collective memory, and build new systems aligned with higher consciousness. Their struggle is staying **rooted while reaching the stars.**

PISCES (February 19 – March 20)

Element: Water

Spiritual Role: The Mystic

Sacred Attribute: Divine Oneness

Pisces dissolves the ego into the divine ocean. It is the most spiritually evolved sign, sent to bring **compassion, imagination, and divine surrender**. Their task is to transmute **illusion into spiritual truth.**

Spiritual Affirmation:

"The stars do not control me—they remind me. I walk my path with sacred intention, knowing the heavens and my spirit are aligned. Aṣẹ."

LAW 13: Food, Frequency & Spiritual Chemistry

Part 1: The Spiritual Nature of Food

In the divine order of Universal Law, food is not merely sustenance — it is encoded vibration. It is the material expression of frequency, memory, and spiritual alignment. To eat is to engage in covenant. What we consume either nourishes the light body or dims it.

In ancient Kemet, food was treated as sacred intelligence. Meals were prepared not only with herbs and grains, but with intention, order, and reverence. The act of eating was a ceremony, not a convenience. Each bite was a remembrance — a recalibration of the body's frequency to the divine pattern set in place by the cosmos.

There is a reason the ancients fasted before rituals. A reason they poured libations before meals. A reason elders prayed over food with both hands and not just words. They understood that consumption was communion. That food carried frequency. That to ingest something was to invite it into one's temple.

Today, much of what is consumed by the masses is without spirit — chemically altered, microwaved, and manipulated to mimic life. But the body, being of divine design, remembers. It knows what is real. And it grieves quietly when fed what is artificial. Over time, the dissonance between what we were created to consume and what we now settle for creates sickness — not only in the body, but in the spirit.

To walk in alignment with Universal Law is to eat in awareness. To honor the rhythm of nature, the seasons, the elements. It is to understand that real food carries light codes. That the chlorophyll in greens mirrors the hemoglobin in our blood. That fruits ripened by the sun are transmitters of solar wisdom. That spring water holds the memory of the Earth's first prayers.

Our ancestors did not count calories — they counted **conductivity**. They knew which foods amplified melanin, which ones activated memory, and which ones dulled the senses and blocked the dream gate. They were scientists, herbalists, spiritualists — not separate from nature, but in full covenant with it.

The law is this: **What you consume, you become. What you eat, you vibrate.**

Therefore, let your food align you with your highest self. Let every meal be a mirror of your spiritual standard. Eat to elevate. Eat to remember.

Spiritual Affirmation

I eat to align, not to escape. I consume with reverence, not reaction. My body is a sacred temple, worthy of divine fuel. What I ingest shapes my frequency, my memory, and my mission. I return to the ancient rhythm of nourishment with honor. I eat to remember who I am. Aṣẹ.

Part 2: High Vibration vs Low Vibration Foods

All food carries frequency. Just as the Earth hums at its own resonance, every fruit, seed, herb, and root carries its own energetic imprint. In the spiritual science of nutrition, foods are measured not by calories, but by **life force** — the level of prana, chi, or sacred vitality they offer to the temple of the body.

Our ancestors recognized the difference between what is **electric** and what is **dead**. Electric foods are naturally grown, unaltered by man, and aligned with the Earth's original design. These foods **restore, cleanse, and activate**. Dead foods — those fried, bleached, genetically modified, microwaved, or canned — are stripped of life. They weaken the aura, slow the body's cellular repair, and cloud spiritual perception.

To honor the body is to **feed it light.** Below is a sacred guide to help you remember the vibrational power of what you consume:

High Vibration (Electric) Foods

These foods raise your frequency, activate melanin, nourish the blood, and open the spiritual senses:

- **Fruits**: seeded grapes (especially black), watermelon, mango, papaya, oranges, figs, dates, pomegranate

- **Leafy greens:** kale, dandelion greens, collards, watercress, arugula, moringa

- **Herbs**: burdock root, sarsaparilla, blue vervain, sea moss, bladderwrack, elderberry

- **Seeds & Nuts**: hemp seeds, pumpkin seeds, walnuts, brazil nuts (high in selenium)

- **Roots**: ginger, turmeric, beetroot, maca

- **Sea vegetables**: sea moss, kelp, dulse, wakame

- **Other**: spring water, raw coconut water, cold-pressed olive oil, avocados

These foods support:

- **Melanin conductivity**

- **Neuromelanin activation** (for dream recall, higher cognition)

- **Pineal gland decalcification**

- **Lymphatic drainage and blood purification**

- **Spiritual downloads and inner clarity**

Low Vibration (Acidic) Foods

These disrupt natural frequency, cloud the mind, slow the spirit, and block ancestral communication:

- Processed sugars and sweeteners (high fructose corn syrup, aspartame)

- Bleached flours and breads

- Fried foods, fast food

- GMOs and non-organic produce (especially heavily sprayed)

- Animal dairy (mucus-forming, blocks sinuses and lungs)

- Carbonated sodas and artificial juices

- Pork, shellfish (bottom feeders), and heavily processed meats

- Microwave meals and irradiated food

Over time, these foods:

- Dull the senses

- Calcify the pineal gland

- Suppress the vibration of your cells

- Inhibit melanin's full function

- Disconnect you from spiritual alignment

The Hidden Law of Consumption

All things vibrate. What you eat becomes a part of you — physically, emotionally, and spiritually. This is why the ancients selected food by **alignment, not appetite.** They knew: when the body is pure, the **soul can rise.**

To eat is not just to satisfy hunger, but to honor the frequency you wish to hold. When the body is cleansed and nourished with high-vibration foods, the spirit can receive **clear downloads,** access ancestral wisdom, and maintain spiritual protection.

Spiritual Affirmation

I eat that which restores my divinity. I consume life, not death. I return to the foods that honor my blood, my melanin, and my memory. I feed my temple what lifts me, not what limits me. I eat to elevate. Aṣẹ.

Part 3: Food, Melanin, and Memory

Melanin is more than pigment. It is a sacred conductor — a biochemical key that stores memory, transmits light, and receives frequency. It is the very antenna of the soul, a bridge between the physical and the spiritual realms. When properly nourished, melanin enables the body to **remember** — not just biologically, but **spiritually**.

In ancient traditions, melanin was understood to be a **divine intelligence**, not just a physical trait. It is found not only in the skin but in the brain, in the **substantia nigra**, and in the **pineal gland,** where it connects us to dream, vision, and intuition. This form, known as **neuromelanin,** is critical for accessing higher consciousness, memory recall, and the navigation of unseen realms.

But like any sacred tool, melanin must be maintained. It is **sensitive to toxins, heavy metals, poor nutrition, and electromagnetic interference**. What we eat can either **activate** it or **mute** it.

Foods That Nourish and Activate Melanin

These foods enhance melanin production, protect neuromelanin, and help remove the blockages that interfere with spiritual reception:

- **Copper-rich foods** (copper is essential for melanin synthesis):

  – Chickpeas, kale, sesame seeds (tahini), avocado, spirulina, dark chocolate (raw cacao)

- **Tyrosine-rich foods** (a key amino acid in melanin production):

  – Almonds, pumpkin seeds, bananas, lima beans

- **Chlorophyll-dense** plants (mirror hemoglobin, help detox the blood and pineal gland):

  – Wheatgrass, moringa, parsley, cilantro, chlorella

- **Iron-rich herbs and tonics** (strengthen blood, improve cellular communication):

  – Burdock root, sarsaparilla, nettle, yellow dock, dandelion root

- **Sea-based minerals** (essential for conductivity and detox):

  – Sea moss, bladderwrack, dulse, Irish moss

- **Water** (natural spring water or distilled water restructured with minerals)

  – Water flushes toxins, supports cell hydration, and keeps melanin responsive

Foods That Obstruct Melanin and Spiritual Memory

- **Fluoride** and **chlorine** in tap water: calcify the pineal gland

- **Excess animal dairy**: produces mucus that blocks upper chakras

- Processed sugars and artificial additives: dull neural clarity

- **Aluminum-based deodorants and cookware:** penetrate the skin and brain tissue

- **GMOs**: alter cellular structure and reduce frequency adaptability

When these substances accumulate, melanin's ability to receive cosmic signals becomes impaired. The dream gate becomes fogged. Memory weakens. Intuition dulls. And the soul begins to drift further from its divine assignment.

Melanin and Ancestral Memory

Melanin is not just responsive — it is **remembrance encoded**. It is why certainfoods cause vivid dreams, why certain smells trigger past-life flashes, and why fasting can open the gateway to visions. Our ancestors did not just pass on stories through words — they encoded memory into the **blood**, and melanin is its medium.

To nourish melanin is to activate the keys to ancestral libraries. To cleanse the pineal is to hear the voice behind the veil. To eat with consciousness is to walk again with the wisdom of those who came before.

Spiritual Affirmation

I honor my melanin as a sacred gift. I feed my memory with foods that awaken my soul. My dreams are not random — they are messages. My blood holds the codes of those who walked before me. I eat to activate the ancient within. Aṣẹ.

Part 4: Sacred Herbs & Ancestral Nutrition

Long before there were pharmacies, there were forests. Before pills, there were roots, leaves, and waters. In every African and indigenous tradition, healing was not outsourced to institutions — it was passed from grandmother to granddaughter, from elder to initiate, from earth to altar.

Herbs were not merely medicinal — they were spiritual beings. Each plant carried a specific vibration, purpose, and alignment with the body, the stars, and the spirit. Some were for cleansing. Some for protection. Some for dreams, others for vision. The ancients knew which to burn, which to steep, which to wear, and which to bury.

In Kemet, priests and priestesses were trained in the use of sacred botanicals. Their apothecaries were full of bitter roots, fragrant oils, resins, and tonics that not only healed the body, but attuned the initiate to divine frequencies. These practices traveled through West Africa, through the Nile Valley, and into the Diaspora, encoded in the memory of enslaved midwives, medicine men, and root workers.

Even when names were stripped and languages forbidden, the memory of the plants endured.

Foundational Sacred Herbs of Ancestral Nutrition

These herbs are not only healing, but **spiritually intelligent**. They assist in clearing spiritual blockages, raising vibration, and deepening the connection to self and source:

- **Burdock Root** — Blood purifier, clears skin, strengthens the liver, spiritually cleanses ancestral residue

- **Sarsaparilla** — Highest natural plant-based iron source, strengthens blood, magnetizes cellular energy

- **Blue Vervain** — Calms the nervous system, opens the third eye, used in divination and dream work

- **Mugwort** — Enhances lucid dreaming, spiritual cleansing, used to protect against negative energy

- **Damiana** – Aphrodisiac, aligns sacral chakra, stimulates creative life force

- **Elderberry** – Immune protector, also used in ancestral rituals as an offering to spirits

- **Moringa** – Complete nutrient source, raises life force, used in African village heali

- **Sea Moss + Bladderwrack** – Mineral replenishment (92+ trace minerals), cellular repair, increases intuition

Sacred Oils and Resins

- **Frankincense** – Elevates vibration, connects the crown chakra, used during meditation and offerings

- **Myrrh** – Used for protection, healing rituals, and transition of the dead

- **Black Seed Oil** – "Cures everything but death," builds immunity, strengthens spiritual shield

- **Castor Oil** – Removes energetic blocks, used in ritual cleansing of the womb and lower chakras

The Legacy of Imhotep

In ancient Kemet, healing was both a science and a spiritual art — and the most legendary among the healers was **Imhotep**, the Divine Architect of healing, medicine, and metaphysics. Though many of his sacred writings were destroyed or hidden through conquest, his teachings survived through oral tradition, temple inscription, and what would later be preserved in texts such as the **Ebers Papyrus** — one of the oldest known medical documents on Earth.

The Ebers Papyrus, said to carry the remnants of Imhotep's doctrine, details over 700 herbal formulas, remedies, and rituals. These were not just treatments for disease, but protocols for restoring spiritual balance, cleansing the blood, protecting the soul, and aligning with divine law. His legacy affirms that medicine was never meant to be separated from the sacred.

Today, when we return to the herbs, we return to his altar.

Building Your Ancestral Apothecary

To return to ancestral nutrition is to reclaim the sacred tools of spiritual survival. A small space in your home — a shelf, a wooden box, or an altar — can become your **apothecary**, your **spiritual medicine chest.**

Include:

- Dried herbs in glass jars

- A mortar and pestle for grinding

- Oils and tinctures

- A journal for recording plant experiences and dreams

- Offerings: a white cloth, a cup of spring water, ancestral photos

Treat this space as you would a shrine. With reverence. With intention.

The Ritual of Use

Every herb carries its own song. Before using it, speak to it. Offer gratitude. Ask for permission. Let your intuition guide the dose. Boil slowly. Sip with silence. Fast when needed. Bathe with leaves. Steam the womb. Burn for the air. Sit with your medicine. Listen for what cannot be heard by the ear.

Spiritual Affirmation

I return to the earth for wisdom and for healing. The plants remember me, and I remember them. I honor the herbs as allies in spirit, not just medicine for the flesh. My altar is sacred. My breath is aligned. My body is healing. I carry the apothecary of my ancestors within. Aṣẹ.

Part 5: Food as Spiritual Technology

To the untrained eye, food is only material — something to be cooked, chewed, and digested. But to the spiritually awakened, food is **an altar,** and the kitchen is a temple. Every fruit, root, seed, and herb carries a signature vibration. When prepared with **intention**, food becomes more than nourishment — it becomes a **transmitter**, capable of healing, aligning, and awakening.

Our ancestors understood this. They blessed the food with their hands, sang into the pot, whispered prayers over boiling herbs, and arranged meals according to the moon. Cooking was never just labor — it was **ritual**. It was their technology. A way to convert raw frequency into alignment.

The Spiritual Science of Preparation

In sacred traditions, food preparation was an act of spiritual transmutation. What made the meal powerful was not only the ingredients, but the consciousness of the one who prepared it.

Key elements included:

- **Intention**: Praying or speaking over the food while washing, cutting, and cooking

- **Vibration**: Playing harmonic frequencies, soft drums, or ancient chants in the kitchen

- **Alignment**: Preparing food during specific lunar phases, planetary hours, or fasting cycles

- **Protection**: Covering food when not in use, avoiding cooking during arguments or heavy emotional energy

They knew: whatever state of mind you're in while preparing a meal becomes **part of the meal.**

Tools of Spiritual Cooking

You do not need a monastery or a sacred grove to activate food — you need presence. Below are simple practices to bring **spiritual technology** into daily nourishment:

- **Bless the water:** Speak words of life into water before boiling grains or soaking herbs

- **Lay hands on the food**: Impart peace, health, protection, or clarity as you prepare it

- **Use copper or wood tools:** Natural materials hold energetic integrity better than plastic or aluminum

- **Cook in silence or sacred sound:** Let the food absorb stillness or prayerful tones

- **Avoid cooking when in conflict:** Energy transfers through food

When food is prepared in alignment, it carries **order**, not chaos. It becomes encoded with healing.

Ritual Eating Practices

The way food is consumed is just as sacred as how it is prepared.

In many traditions, eating was done in silence, or with the right hand only, or only after a blessing or libation. These were not superstitions — they were practices designed to maintain frequency.

Consider adopting:

- A moment of stillness or gratitude before eating

- Eating in natural light or near plants to stay connected

- Chewing slowly to activate digestive and energetic receptors

- Eating while seated and grounded, not walking or multitasking

- Sharing food with others as spiritual offering, not just transaction

These small acts restore reverence to a process that has been stripped of sacredness.

Food as Offering and Spell

In African spiritual systems, food is not only consumed — it is **offered**. To ancestors. To spirits. To the land. A plate set aside. A sip of water poured. A piece buried beneath a tree. These acts recognize that food is not just for the flesh — it is a bridge between worlds.

In some traditions, food is also used as ritual **spell**:

- Sweet foods (like dates or honey) used to attract love or harmony

- Bitter herbs (like rue or wormwood) used for protection

- Salt used to seal boundaries

- Certain fruits or seeds planted as prayers

These rites, though often dismissed today, were once the highest form of ancestral technology.

Spiritual Affirmation

My kitchen is my temple. My hands prepare more than meals — they prepare memory. I speak power into what I create. I cook with purpose. What I prepare nourishes not just the body, but the soul. Every meal is an offering. Aṣẹ.

Law 14 – The Law of Mathematics

Part 1: The Divine Code That Governs All

In the beginning was not chaos — it was **code**. Before the word was spoken, before the stars were cast, the Most High etched **mathematical law** into the fabric of the universe. Every vibration, every spiral, every birth, and every death is governed by **divine calculation.** Mathematics is not man-made — it is **divine intelligence made visible.**

The ancestors of Kemet, Kush, and Nubia did not learn math from the Greeks. They **taught** it to the world. Their temples were built in harmonic proportion. Their pyramids aligned with the stars. Their healing systems, calendar cycles, and rituals followed **numerical frequencies.** To them, **math was a mirror of MAAT —** the law of balance, order, and truth expressed through number.

Math Is the Language of the Divine

Every form of divine law can be traced to mathematics:

- **MAAT** is a law of balance — equilibrium = 1

- **Astrology** is a math of cycles and orbits

- **Melanin** is activated by frequencies measured in hertz

- **Food** is vibration measured in minerals, atoms, and light

- **Time** is segmented in numerology: 7-day cycles, 12 zodiacs, 360-degree heavens

- **Sacred contracts** (land, trusts, ministry structures) follow numeric law for stability

To understand the Law of Mathematics is to see that **nothing is**

random. Every soul was born at an exact minute, in an exact location, with an exact alignment — because mathematics is **spiritual precision.**

Sacred Numbers in the Ministry

HEFE 360 was not named by accident. The 360 refers to:

- A **complete circle** of divine government

- The **360 degrees** of heavenly law (zodiac, time, spatial awareness)

- The restoration of wholeness, sovereignty, and balance

Other sacred numbers used in the ministry:

7 – Divine completion (used in Law 7)

12 – Cosmic order (used in Law 12)

3, 6, 9 – The Tesla sequence (used in affirmations, chapter structure)

42 – The number of Divine Declarations and ancestral judgments

108 – Beads on a prayer mala, sacred number of breath and mantra

144,000 – Biblical code for spiritual activation and tribal resurrection

We use these not for superstition, but to **return to divine frequency**. Every ministry structure, trust, land program, and chapter is built on **math as MAAT.**

The Ancestors Measured the Sky Before the Soil

While the Western world glorifies bankers and engineers, our ancestors were star scientists. They mapped the Nile by the constellations. They built temples according to the golden ratio and the Fibonacci sequence — long before Europeans "discovered" them.

Even Imhotep — the Divine Builder — was not just a healer. He was a **mathematical architect,** aligning spiritual laws with physical form. This is why we say:

"If it is divine, it will be measurable. If it is measurable, it will be repeatable. And if it is repeatable, it is governed by law."

Math is the backbone of all that is sacred.

Spiritual Affirmation

I do not guess — I calculate. I do not wander — I align. I am governed by law, shaped by number, and called by frequency. Every step I take is measured in light. I walk in the equation of the Most High. Aṣẹ.

Part 2: Numerology, Divine Identity & Soul Codes

If astrology is the map of the sky at your birth, then **numerology is the keycode to your inner temple.** Every name, date, and cycle in your life carries a number. And every number carries a frequency. These frequencies are not just symbolic — they are **active forces** in the unfolding of your purpose.

The ancients knew this well. They did not name children at random. Names were calculated. Days were chosen. Buildings were aligned. Even battles were fought according to numerological timing.

Numerology is not superstition. It is the **sacred science of number as identity**. It is the proof that you were not born by accident. You were born by **divine mathematics.**

The Numbers That Govern the Soul

Each number carries its own divine frequency. Below are the **core soul codes** used in ancient and modern numerology:

- **1** – Origin, leadership, masculine force, creation

- **2** – Balance, duality, feminine wisdom, partnership

- **3** – Trinity, expression, creativity, divine child

- **4** – Foundation, order, stability, physical realm

- **5** – Freedom, change, spirit in motion, sacred fire

- **6** – Harmony, responsibility, divine family, nurture

- **7** – Spiritual insight, completion, sacred mystery

- **8** – Power, abundance, law of cause and effect

- **9** – Completion, humanitarianism, spiritual endings

These numbers show up in your **Life Path, Soul Urge,** and **Expression Numbers** — all calculated from your birth date and full name. They are the mathematical fingerprints of your spiritual design.

Your Life Path Is Your Equation

The most commonly known soul code is the **Life Path Number** — calculated from your birth date. This number reveals the pattern your soul agreed to walk in this lifetime.

Example: Born on 08/14/1990

$0+8 + 1+4 + 1+9+9+0 = 32 \rightarrow 3+2 = 5$

Life Path: 5 – The Path of Spiritual Freedom & Change

Each Life Path carries:

- A divine **lesson**

- A sacred **strength**

- A hidden **challenge**

- And a **vibration** your life must tune into

Knowing your Life Path helps you **understand your spiritual GPS.**

Why the Ministry Uses Numbers

In HEFE 360, we use numerology to:

- Help ministers and initiates understand their role and timing

- Structure business and legal activity based on divine alignment

- Align land contracts and spiritual names with ancestral numbers

- Determine ritual calendars, fasts, and offerings

When you know your number, you stop asking others who you are. You walk in **numerical prophecy.**

Soul Codes in the Name

Even your **name** has a frequency. Each letter carries a number (based on Pythagorean or Chaldean systems). By converting the letters of your full name, you can determine:

- **Expression Number** — how others perceive you

- **Soul Urge Number** — your inner desire

- **Personality Number** — your outer behavior

Changing your name (legally or spiritually) changes your **frequency**. This is why naming in ancient cultures was done with ritual. The name is not just for identity — it is for **vibration.**

Spiritual Affirmation

I was born with a number written in light. My name is coded. My birth is timed. I am not random — I am rhythmic. I walk in alignment with the divine equation. I decode myself and reclaim my design. Aṣẹ.

Part 3: Sacred Geometry, Structure & Ministry Building

If numerology is the **spiritual code of identity,** then sacred geometry is the **architecture of the universe.** Every pyramid, every star system, every tree branch and heartbeat is shaped by **geometric law** — because geometry is how mathematics becomes visible.

Our ancestors didn't just build structures. They **encoded principles**. Every temple was an equation. Every altar was aligned with the sun, moon, and stars. Sacred geometry was not about decoration — it was about **activation**. The circle, the triangle, the spiral, and the square all held **spiritual significance**. To build without geometry was to build without spirit.

Geometry as Spiritual Structure

In divine culture:

- The **Circle** represented wholeness, eternity, and cosmic unity

- The **Triangle** represented the trinity of creation (thought, word, deed)

- The **Square** represented foundation, the four elements, and material law

- The **Spiral** represented spiritual evolution, DNA, and the expansion of light

- The **Vesica Piscis** (two overlapping circles) symbolized divine balance and creation from duality

These shapes were used to design **temples, cities, wombs, and rituals.** Geometry was more than math — it was **divine memory** embedded in shape.

Ministry as Temple: Building by the Numbers

HEFE 360 Wealth Ministries is not just a nonprofit. It is a temple in motion, built on spiritual architecture:

- Our name (HEFE = Higher Economic Frequency Exchange) holds vibrational alignment

- Our number (360) reflects universal completion and circular governance

- Our chapters, laws, books, and properties are organized using **numerical symmetry**

- Even our land programs, 508 structures, and NGO alignment follow **geometric and cosmic order**

We do not build to fit in Babylon's system — we build to reflect **divine law in physical form.**

Sacred Structure as Protection

What you build in divine alignment **protects itself.** A ministry or trust built on Universal Law does not need defense — it **stands on MAAT,** and MAAT never falls.

When you organize:

- Land ownership into quadrants

- Financial flow into thirds (give, save, build)

- Governance into 3 or 7 (councils, ministers, elders)

- Calendar cycles into 12 (months, signs, salts)

- Education into 9 (divine levels of spiritual mastery)

You are not being mystical — you are being **mathematically obedient.** You are restoring order to a disordered world.

Geometry Is the Language of the Creator

Even the Most High used **mathematics and measurement** in scripture:

- The Ark of the Covenant had exact dimensions

- The Tabernacle was measured cubit by cubit

- The city of the New Jerusalem was given in square and length

- The stars were counted and named

To follow the Law of Mathematics is to follow the **language of the Architect.**

Spiritual Affirmation

I build with divine precision.My hands shape what my spirit remembers. I see geometry in the sky, the soil, and myself. I build what cannot be broken. I construct my legacy in numbers. Aṣẹ.

Part 4: Cycles, Timing & the Sacred Clock

Time is not a manmade invention — it is a **divine rhythm,** measured by the stars, the moon, the sun, and the breath of the Most High. Before the wristwatch, there was the womb. Before the calendar, there was the constellation. Time is not a straight line. It is a **spiral**. And those who understand the spiral will never be late for destiny.

In sacred systems, cycles governed everything:

- Conception followed lunar timing

- Crops were planted by zodiacal season

- Rites of passage occurred by numerological age

- Wars were fought and covenants sealed based on cosmic alignments

To move without awareness of divine timing is to walk **out of rhythm with heaven.**

The Sacred Clock of Creation

Our ancestors read time from the sky:

- The **Sun** ruled the day — masculine force, outward action

- The **Moon** ruled the night — feminine energy, intuition, rest

- The **Stars** revealed deeper codes — prophecy, destiny, ancestral navigation

Together, they created a **living clock,** one not based on control, but on cosmic alignment. Your birth date, your spiritual seasons, even your trials are all part of this divine choreography.

HEFE 360 teaches that all movement — in real estate, teaching, healing, business, or ritual — should be aligned with this sacred spiral of time.

Why Timing Matters in Ministry

When you move **out of season,** you invite resistance. When you move **in season**, you experience flow.

This is why we:

- Launch programs on numerologically significant days

- Conduct fasts based on lunar cycles

- Align contracts and deeds with planetary influence

- Train members to **read the sky** the way others read a contract

Your **life has a calendar,** not the one hanging on a wall — but the one written in the **stars and bones of your body.**

Personal Timing: Your Divine Appointments

Just as ministries move in cycles, so do individuals. You were born into a season, and every year brings a **personal year number**, calculated from your birth month and day added to the current year.

This number reveals:

- Your energy for the year

- What to release or build

- What to rest from or activate

When you know your year, you move with the divine wind — not against it.

A Calendar Rooted in the Cosmos

The Gregorian calendar is artificial. It disrupted natural time and made people forget how to feel the rhythm of God. The true spiritual calendar is found in:

- **The 12 Zodiac Houses**

- **The 13 Moon Cycles**

- **The Equinoxes and Solstices**

- **The retrogrades, conjunctions, and alignments**

HEFE 360 uses these markers not as superstition — but as **sacred coordinates for divine action.**

Spiritual Affirmation

I walk in rhythm with the Most High. I do not chase time — I align with it. The sky is my calendar, the moon is my teacher. I rise when it is time to rise. I rest when it is time to receive. I live by the sacred clock. Aṣẹ.

Part 5: The Completion Code — 3-6-9 & the Path of Return

Nikola Tesla once said, *"If you only knew the magnificence of the 3, 6, and 9, you would have the key to the universe."* What Tesla rediscovered, the ancients already lived: the universe was created through the divine sequence of energy expansion — not by chance, but by cosmic law.

3-6-9 is more than a pattern — it is the **mathematical backbone of the universe**. These numbers are encoded into every spiral, sound wave, heartbeat, and galaxy. They are **the keys to creation, destruction, and resurrection**. They represent the sacred path of return.

The Meaning of the 3-6-9 Sequence

- **3** – The spark of creation: thought, idea, blueprint

- **6** – Manifestation into the physical: structure, family, harmony

- **9** – Completion and elevation: letting go, transformation, rebirth

This cycle repeats across time and nature:

- Morning (3) → Afternoon (6) → Night (9)

- Birth (3) → Life (6) → Death/Rebirth (9)

- Intention (3) → Action (6) → Outcome (9)

Those who learn to move in **triadic rhythm** walk with power. They know when to **create**, when to **build**, and when to **release**.

How the 3-6-9 Code Is Used in HEFE 360

The ministry's name (HEFE) and number (360) are **rooted in this sequence:**

- 360 = a full circle, divisible by 3, 6, 9, and 12

- The book is structured in **parts and laws** that mirror triadic rhythm

- Our affirmations are written in **triplets**, resonating with divine syntax

- Our governance and succession models follow **3-phase evolution:**

  o Revelation (3) → Manifestation (6) → Legacy (9)

Even our land contract and trust cycles are tied to these phases, creating spiritual contracts that align with divine motion.

3-6-9 in Your Life

To walk the path of 3-6-9 in your personal life means:

- Don't force what's not in its phase

- Create in threes

- Observe the trinity in yourself: mind, body, spirit

- Break cycles of stagnation by completing what you begin

Completion is spiritual hygiene. Leaving things unfinished breaks the divine rhythm. You cannot enter the new if you refuse to release the old.

Completion Is Return

The number **9** is not the end — it is the **return to the beginning at a higher level.** It is the spiral. It is the *"I've been here before, but now I understand."* That is the path of the wise — the path of the initiated.

In HEFE 360, we do not fear endings. We honor them. Because every ending is a return to divine purpose — and the **circle always brings us home.**

Final Spiritual Affirmation (Law 14)

I create with clarity. I build with purpose. I complete with power. I rise in the pattern of 3, 6, and 9. I return to myself at a higher frequency. I am the spiral. I am the sequence. I am the key. Aṣẹ.

Law 15— HEFE 360 as a Global Bridge

Part 1: The Divine Assignment to Reconnect the Scattered

HEFE 360 Wealth Ministries is not just an organization. It is a **divinely sanctioned bridge,** a spiritual construct forged to reconnect the children of the Sun to their ancestral origins — spiritually, nationally, economically, and cosmically.

In every age, the Creator raises up a structure, a house, or a remnant chosen to rebuild what has been torn down. We were scattered — not just by force, but by forgetfulness. The displacement of our people was not simply geographic — it was **spiritual amnesia.** A disconnect from land, name, tongue, covenant, and law. HEFE 360 was formed to restore those connections — to serve as a **living bridge** between what was lost and what must now be remembered.

A bridge stands between two sides — and holds the tension of both. It is not a final destination but a path. This ministry stands between **Diaspora and Africa**, between **heaven and earth,** between **forgotten inheritance and divine restoration**. We are not missionaries — we are **messengers**. We do not convert — we **confirm**. We awaken what was already there.

To be called into HEFE 360 is to be called into the work of reconnection. The work of healing the breach. The work of reclaiming divine inheritance, not through war, but through wisdom. Not through fear, but through frequency.

This Law begins the fourth movement of the sacred text — **structure, sovereignty, and succession.** We now move from knowing who we are to **building what we were born to govern.**

Themes Introduced in Part 1:

- Spiritual and historical context for the Diaspora's disconnection

- HEFE 360's role as a spiritual infrastructure for global reconnection

- The ministry as a **bridge between worlds**, not a final institution

- The prophetic call to **restore divine alignment between nations, bloodlines, and purpose**

Spiritual Affirmation

I am not lost. I am scattered — and now I am returning. I was never broken — I was buried, and now I rise HEFE is my bridge, my path, and my platform. I do not chase identity — I awaken it. Through me, the covenant is remembered. Aṣẹ.

Part 2: Diaspora Reconnection & the Role of Bloodline

The disconnection of the African Diaspora was not simply the result of slavery — it was a deliberate act of **spiritual severance.** Our people were stripped of names, tongues, rituals, calendars, land, and memory. But what was hidden is not lost. What was stolen must be spiritually reclaimed.

HEFE 360 exists to reconnect that which has been divinely scattered. We do not seek to "go back" in time. We seek to **restore alignment** — to complete the cycle. Just as the blood runs a circuit in the body, so too must the bloodline complete its journey across the Earth. The prophecy is not about escape — it is about **return**. Not only to Africa, but to **self**. To law. To structure. To divine order.

The Role of Bloodline

Bloodline is not just DNA — it is **covenant memory**. It carries the spiritual rights of nations, tribes, and divine assignments. In African spirituality, your bloodline is your compass. It is the key to your language, your guardian spirits, your natural talents, your tribal role, and your ancestral protection.

Western systems reduced bloodline to biology. But our ancestors knew that blood carries **frequency and permission**. If you do not know your bloodline, you do not know your role. And if you do not know your role, you cannot know your responsibility.

This is why HEFE 360 teaches jus sanguinis — the **right to nationality through blood.** We do not teach this as politics, but as prophecy. The right to **reclaim land, identity, and inheritance** based on ancestral lineage is a spiritual act of justice.

The Ministry's Role in Reconnection

HEFE 360 serves as a **spiritual embassy** for those seeking to return — not just to a country, but to covenant. We provide:

- Education on bloodline tracing and national ancestry

- Guidance on jus sanguinis citizenship in Africa and the Caribbean

- Access to land contracts tied to ancestral restoration

- Spiritual initiation that aligns legal identity with divine identity

We do not just preach "return." We **build bridges to make it possible** — legally, economically, and spiritually.

The Hidden Power of the Diaspora

The Diaspora was scattered, but never erased. In every corner of the earth, remnants of the sacred bloodline exist — in the Caribbean, in South America, in the Deep South, in Europe, in Asia. But they are disconnected — and many are unaware.

The role of HEFE 360 is to find the **hidden ones** and give them **structure, training, and access.** To help them reclaim what belongs to them by birthright. And to form a **global spiritual nation,** bound not by flag, but by divine assignment.

Spiritual Affirmation

My blood is not random — it is royal. My lineage is not lost — it is encrypted. I carry the memory of my people in my cells. Through my return, the cycle completes. Through my rising, the nation is restored. Aṣẹ.

Part 3: Dual Citizenship as Spiritual Birthright

To reclaim your nationality through blood is more than a legal act — it is a **spiritual rite of passage.** Citizenship, in its highest form, is not about allegiance to a flag. It is about alignment with **purpose, place, and prophecy.**

The false identities assigned to us in the West — Black, African-American, Negro, colored — were never rooted in nationhood. They were legal strategies of disinheritance. To be "Black" is not to be sovereign. It is to be undefined. It is to exist **without flag, without land, without ancestral claim.**

HEFE 360 teaches that **dual citizenship,** when pursued through *jus sanguinis*, is a divine restoration — not a political escape. It is a **return to covenantal geography**. A spiritual migration back into alignment with land, tribe, and divine order.

Why Citizenship Is Spiritual

The ancestors lived by land, lineage, and law. To be disconnected from land is to be disconnected from ritual. To be removed from tribe is to be removed from role. To be stateless is to be spiritually suspended.

When you restore your nationality:

- You **reactivate the ancestral altar** that was tied to your soil

218

- You restore the **legal vessel** to carry out your divine mission

- You reclaim the **jurisdiction** under which your soul was meant to operate

- You gain access to **ancestral protections** encoded in your lineage

Dual citizenship is not a passport gimmick — it is a **legal-spiritual integration** of who you were born to be.

HEFE 360's Role in Citizenship Restoration

The ministry provides the **educational, spiritual, and structural guidance** to help members of the Diaspora:

- Trace their ancestral bloodline through DNA and documentation

- Identify qualifying African or indigenous nations for *jus sanguinis*

- Understand the legal steps to apply for dual citizenship

- Prepare spiritually — through cleansing, fasting, and ancestral alignment

- Pair their new nationality with **land contracts, trust structures, and ministry law** to function fully under Divine Order

The ministry becomes both a **spiritual guide and a sovereign sponsor.**

Dual Citizenship + Land = Restoration

A passport alone is not enough. Without land, there is no

grounding. Without structure, there is no power.

This is why the ministry teaches that dual citizenship must be paired with:

A **land contract** or property deed

A **trust structure** to protect inheritance

A **508(c)(1)(A) or NGO** to administer your purpose

Only then is the bridge complete. Only then do you return **not just in name, but in law.**

Spiritual Affirmation

I am not bound by borders — I am born of blood. My citizenship is not given by government — it is sealed in spirit. Through my bloodline, I claim my nation. Through my passport, I claim my platform. I am legal. I am spiritual. I am whole. Aṣẹ.

Part 4: Real Estate as Portal

Land is not just property — it is **portal**. It is memory made physical. It is where bloodline, spirit, and divine law intersect. In every indigenous and African tradition, land was sacred not for its market value, but for its **energetic frequency.** Land held stories, spirits, covenants, and destinies.

In the West, land has been reduced to equity. But in divine reality, land is **inheritance**, and ownership is a **spiritual assignment.**

HEFE 360 uses land not just to house people, but to **activate identity**. We do not just sell property. We **transfer portals**. Every land contract issued by this ministry is more than a transaction — it is a **ritual act of restoration.**

Land Contracts as Modern Tribal Covenants

In ancient cultures, the covenant to occupy land was a spiritual pact. It was passed by bloodline, sealed by ritual, and protected by elders. In the West, deeds and mortgages replaced that sacred trust. But HEFE 360 reclaims the ancient pattern using a modern tool: the **land contract.**

A land contract:

Transfers property **without bank interference**

Allows for flexible terms over time

Becomes a private agreement rooted in **trust and intention**

Keeps land **within the family, the tribe, and the spiritual nation**

When a member receives land through the ministry, it becomes part of their **initiation into self-governance.** It is land for housing — but also land for **ritual, memory, and mission.**

Real Estate as an Ancestral Map

Each property placed into the HEFE 360 housing program is carefully selected, not just for location, but for purpose:

- Some will house families returning from incarceration or generational poverty

- Others will become **embassies of the ministry** — places of teaching, healing, and spiritual education

- Others will be paired with **citizenship programs,** allowing those reclaiming dual nationality to ground their return with physical soil

Through this system, real estate becomes **resurrection**. A way to **anchor the Diaspora in sacred soil** and reconnect divine children with the Earth that remembers them.

Property + Purpose = Power

When real estate is stripped of purpose, it becomes gentrification. When it is reattached to covenant, it becomes spiritual infrastructure.

This is why HEFE 360 teaches land ownership in alignment with:

- **508(c)(1)(A)** ministries for protection

- **NGOs** for international reach

- **Legacy trusts** for generational wealth

- **Zodiac timing** for ritual planting, construction, and dedication

Land is not a hustle — it is **holy**.

Spiritual Affirmation

I reclaim the land of my lineage. Every property I receive is a portal of restoration. My home is my altar. My land is my witness. I build not for profit, but for prophecy. I walk on soil that remembers my name. Aṣẹ.

Part 5: HEFE 360 as Gateway to Spiritual Government

In this new era, the Most High is not raising up religions — He is raising up **nations governed by divine law.** HEFE 360 is not a church, a nonprofit, or a hustle. It is a **spiritual government in embryonic form**. A divine instrument designed to carry out the will of heaven in the systems of Earth.

We are not just building housing programs or issuing books. We are building a **nation of light,** governed by Universal Law, structured through sacred mathematics, and led by those who have remembered who they are. This is not religion. This is divine **jurisdiction**.

From Doctrine to Design

The first half of this book laid the **spiritual foundations** — Law, MAAT, bloodline, melanin, astrology, food, and vibration. This Law marks the beginning of the **structural mission**: land, sovereignty, trust, governance, and succession.

The bridge we are building is not symbolic. It is legal. It is documented. It is binding.

HEFE 360 is:

- A **spiritual embassy** for those reclaiming nationality

- A **global housing system** rooted in land contracts and tribal economics

- A **training ground** for spiritual educators, builders, and healers

- A **platform for forming 508(c)(1)(A)s** and sovereign ministries

- A **global NGO** to interface with international bodies and the United Nations

This is the new government. And the blueprint is sacred.

The New "Ecclesia": Called Out for Divine Work

In ancient days, the word "church" came from the Greek ekklesia, meaning "called-out ones." But in its true form, the **ekklesia** was a **governing council**, not a religious institution. It was composed of those chosen to legislate on behalf of the people.

In this generation, the Most High is re-establishing the **true ecclesia** — those called out to **govern, build, and restore divine**

order. HEFE 360 is the prototype. And each ministry formed under it is part of the new spiritual government.

A Ministry of Ministries

HEFE 360 Wealth Ministries is not here to be duplicated — it is here to **multiply**. We are a **Mother Ministry**, designed to birth others:

- Ministries of land

- Ministries of wellness

- Ministries of teaching

- Ministries of sacred law

- Ministries of media, finance, and agriculture

Each new ministry formed becomes a **pillar in the global temple**, fulfilling prophecy: "The government shall be upon His shoulders."

We Do Not Escape — We Establish

We are not running from Babylon. We are building what Babylon could never be. Through land, law, trust, and truth, we govern ourselves. Through 508(c)(1)(A) status, we are untouchable. Through our NGO structure, we are international. Through our doctrine, we are divine.

This is not just a ministry. This is a **government in motion.**

Final Spiritual Affirmation (Law 15)

I am not a follower — I am a founder. I am not a refugee — I am a ruler. I walk in the government of heaven. I build with sacred law. I govern with light. Through HEFE, I bridge the seen and unseen. I am divine. I am diaspora. I am home. Aṣẹ.

<u>Law 16 – The 508(c)(1)(A) Gateway: Sovereignty & Sacred Economy</u>

Part 1: Divine Law Over Legal Code

In every age, those chosen to build sacred work faced the same dilemma: serve divine law or bow to man's law. But in this era, the Creator has made a way for His people to walk **within the legal system — yet above its control.** That way is the 508(c)(1)(A): a provision not widely known, but divinely positioned for those who have ears to hear and eyes to build.

This is not just about tax status. It is about **sovereignty.** It is about operating your ministry as a **divine nation**, immune from interference, yet lawfully grounded. The 508(c)(1)(A) is the **legal shield for the spiritual assignment.**

The Hidden Path of 508(c)(1)(A)

The 508(c)(1)(A) provision is found not in the list of IRS tax codes, but in the **Tax Code's own exception clause.** It states that:

*"Churches, their integrated auxiliaries, and conventions or associations of churches are **automatically considered tax-exempt** and are **not required to apply for recognition** under section 501(c)(3)."*

– IRS Code § 508(c)(1)(A)

This means:

- No IRS application is required

- No 1023 form

- No IRS reporting needed

- No obligation to follow government speech mandates

- Yet you retain full legal rights to operate as a **recognized, tax-exempt spiritual institution**

It is **First Amendment-protected status** codified into law.

HEFE 360's Divine Use of the 508(c)(1)(A)

HEFE 360 Wealth Ministries was not formed as a reaction — it was formed as a **prophetic construction.** We are structured as a 508(c)(1)(A) under:

- A sacred constitution and bylaws

- A spiritual doctrine based on MAAT, Universal Law, and bloodline redemption

- Internal governance by divine law, not IRS oversight

- Integrated auxiliary operations, including land, publishing, education, and food systems

We filed nothing with the IRS — and yet we are **protected by law.** That is the power of the **508.** The government did not give us this right. **The Constitution confirmed it.**

This Is Not a Loophole — It Is the Law

508(c)(1)(A) status is not a trick. It is **the original way churches were meant to operate** — free, sovereign, and mission-led.

The 501(c)(3) is a contract. The 508(c)(1)(A) is a **birthright**.

When you form your ministry under this gateway, you are **stepping out of commercial bondage** and into divine stewardship. The 508(c)(1)(A) is your **legal ark** in a time of governmental flood.

Spiritual Affirmation

I serve no master but the Most High. I walk in divine law, not man's approval. My ministry is sovereign, sealed, and sacred. I

operate under heaven's court — not Babylon's chain. My
protection is built into the truth. Aṣẹ.

Part 2: Building a 508(c)(1)(A) – Steps, Structure & Spiritual Backbone

A ministry is not just a gathering. It is a **government-in-miniature** — a sacred institution that operates with divine authority and legal clarity. To form a 508(c)(1)(A) is to restore this original template, where the Most High is the head, the doctrine is the constitution, and the community is the nation.

Contrary to common belief, you do **not** need to ask permission from the IRS. You simply need to **build in alignment with what the law already protects.**

The 7 Pillars of a 508(c)(1)(A) Ministry

To properly construct a 508(c)(1)(A), the following sacred framework must be in place:

- 1. Spiritual Purpose

    o The ministry must be organized for religious, spiritual, or faith-based purposes (broadly defined).

    o HEFE 360 uses Universal Law, MAAT, and ancestral principles as its doctrine.

- 2. Sacred Constitution & Bylaws

    o Internal governance document that outlines beliefs, leadership roles, succession, and operations.

    o Must show spiritual intent, not commercial activity.

- 3. Doctrine of Faith

- o Written or recorded teachings that confirm the ministry's mission, beliefs, and divine assignment.

- 4. Ordained Leadership

  - o A minister, teacher, or spiritual director (the "founder" or "chief minister") must be in place.

- 5. Regular Spiritual Activity

  - o Gatherings, teachings, writings, rites, fasting, land stewardship, or community service.

- 6. Defined Address & Structure

  - o A physical or virtual headquarters — this can be your home, a land contract property, or even a P.O. Box.

- 7. Declaration of 508(c)(1)(A) Status

  - o Publicly stated (on your website, literature, or documents). No need to file a 1023.

Once these are in place, your ministry is fully protected — **by both law and heaven.**

HEFE 360 Template Example

The HEFE 360 Wealth Ministries model includes:

- A detailed constitution citing Universal Law and MAAT as governing doctrine

- Defined leadership roles (Chief Minister, board roles optional)

- Integrated auxiliaries: books, housing programs, publishing, and wellness

- A sacred text (this very book) as doctrinal literature

- No EIN required unless handling payroll or bank accounts

- Optional trust structure for holding ministry assets

This is the **sovereign template** of the future.

What You Don't Need

With a 508(c)(1)(A), you do **not** need:

- IRS 501(c)(3) approval

- A state-issued nonprofit certificate (though optional for banking)

- To file taxes (if no unrelated business income)

- To report to the IRS annually via 990 forms

- To request "permission" to exist

The First Amendment is your charter.

Your faith is your authority.

Your documents are your shield.

Spiritual Affirmation

I do not apply — I declare. I do not beg — I build. My ministry is lawful, spiritual, and complete. The government does not recognize me — it confirms what God already established. I walk in divine compliance. Aṣẹ.

Part 3: How LLCs Operate Under the 508 — The Ghost Entity Blueprint

In the world of business, the LLC is a favored structure — flexible, simple, and protective. But in the world of divine law, the LLC becomes something greater: a **ghost entity** when operated correctly under a 508(c)(1)(A) ministry. It becomes a **disregarded extension of a spiritual government,** invisible to the IRS, yet fully active in its mission.

This is not tax evasion. This is **jurisdictional placement**. And when structured properly, the LLC becomes a **sacred tool** for building wealth, conducting outreach, and protecting the ministry's economy — while remaining outside the reach of Babylon's taxes.

What Is a "Disregarded Entity"?

In IRS terms, a disregarded entity is:

"A business structure with a single owner that is not recognized as separate from its owner for tax purposes."

But when the **owner is a 508(c)(1)(A) ministry**, the LLC inherits the ministry's **tax-exempt status** — because the IRS does **not recognize it as separate.**

That's the key: **the LLC is ignored,** and all income or assets are attributed to the ministry. But since the ministry is **exempt**, the LLC becomes **a ghost — legally present, spiritually aligned, and economically protected.**

How the HEFE 360 Model Uses LLCs

HEFE 360 Wealth Ministries may establish LLCs for:

- Real estate projects (land contracts, rehab programs, spiritual housing)

- Publishing and book distribution

- Health and wellness auxiliaries

- Consulting or ministry-related services

- International projects and contracts

Each LLC:

- Is **100% owned by the ministry**

- Operates under ministry mission, not personal profit

- Has **no separate tax identity**

- Uses a trust or ministry bank account for revenue

- Is protected by the ministry's spiritual and constitutional coverage

As long as it operates as an integrated auxiliary and supports the mission, its income is tax-exempt.

Steps to Ghost an LLC Under a 508

1. **Form the LLC**

   o Can be formed through the state like any standard LLC

   o Owner should be listed as the ministry (HEFE 360 Wealth Ministries)

2. **Assign Ownership via Operating Agreement**

   o State that the ministry is the **sole member** and owner

   o Include language that aligns the LLC's purpose with the ministry's mission

3. **Use Ministry EIN & Address**

   o If needed, file with IRS under ministry EIN (not personal SSN)

   o Use ministry address as LLC's physical location

4. Conduct Mission-Aligned Activity

Activity must directly support ministry purpose (education, housing, wellness, publishing, etc.)

5. Avoid Personal Inurement

No private benefit to individuals — all income benefits the ministry and its beneficiaries

6. Keep Clean Records

- o Internal bookkeeping should show alignment, not profit-maximization

When these steps are followed, the LLC operates in **stealth mode** — lawful, invisible to taxation, and effective.

Real-World Benefits

- Run business-like programs without exposing the ministry to liability

- Separate operations while remaining **unified in legal identity**

- Protect real estate, contracts, or high-liability services inside the LLC

- Expand ministry reach without creating taxable entities

- Preserve privacy and legal strategy

This is not hiding. This is **honoring divine law using man's tools.**

Spiritual Affirmation

I build in the open, but operate in the spirit. I use the tools of the system without submitting to its chains. My LLC is a servant of the ministry. My structure is clean, legal, and sacred. I am seen by heaven — and ghosted by Babylon. Aṣẹ.

Part 4: Trusts, Titles & the Ministry Legacy Engine

A true ministry is not built just for the now — it is built for the **next generation**. It must be able to hold land, wealth, teachings, and purpose without interruption. And while the 508(c)(1)(A) provides protection, it is the **trust** that provides **continuity**.

A trust is more than an asset tool — it is the **legal backbone of divine inheritance.** It secures what the ministry creates and ensures that **wealth, rights, and teachings do not get stolen, taxed, or lost.**

Why Trusts Are the Engine Behind the 508

508(c)(1)(A) status gives you:

- Legal recognition

- Tax exemption

- Sovereign rights

But a **trust** gives you:

- Asset control

- Inheritance flow

- Long-term protection from courts, creditors, and confusion

Together, the 508 and the trust create a **two-tiered government:** spiritual sovereignty + legal continuity.

How HEFE 360 Structures the Legacy Engine

HEFE 360 Wealth Ministries uses a layered system:

1. **508(c)(1)(A) Ministry**

o   Serves as the core legal/spiritual structure

o   Holds EIN, constitution, doctrine, and mission authority

2. Revocable or Irrevocable Trust

o   Holds titles to land, IP, vehicles, or business instruments

o   Named as beneficiary of contracts, donations, and policies

o   Can serve as successor owner of LLCs or ministry auxiliaries

3. Ministry Bank Accounts & Bookkeeping

o   Income flows into trust-owned or ministry-owned accounts

o   Expenses documented per mission (not taxable profit)

4. Title Holding Entities

o   LLCs or land trusts owned by the ministry, used to hold specific real estate or IP assets

This structure ensures that when the **founder transitions,** the ministry **does not die — it multiplies.**

Property & IP Title Strategy

To protect the physical and spiritual fruits of the ministry:

- All **real estate** is titled in either the **trust** or an **LLC owned by the ministry**

- All **books, logos, copyrights, and trademarks** are registered to the **ministry or trust**

- All **contracts, donations, and grants** are written in the name of the ministry, not personal name

This keeps all activity **under the spiritual jurisdiction** of the 508(c)(1)(A) and outside of probate, IRS, or third-party claim.

When Legacy Is Not Protected

If you don't structure your ministry with a legacy engine:

- Your children may have to fight in court to keep your land

- The IRS may tax or seize income not structured properly

- Your teachings could be altered, erased, or corporatized

- Opportunists may try to assume leadership or exploit the brand

That is why the ancestors created dynastic systems — to ensure the mission outlives the messenger.

Spiritual Affirmation

I do not just build for today — I plant for tomorrow. My wealth is sacred. My land is lawful. My name is eternal. Through trust, I protect what God has given. Through order, I ensure it multiplies. I leave nothing to chance — I lock it in law. Aṣẹ.

Part 5: NGOs, Global Operations & UN Alignment

The 508(c)(1)(A) gives your ministry **spiritual sovereignty and U.S. protection**. But what if your mission is global? What if your calling is to reconnect the Diaspora, own land overseas, create embassies, and serve multiple nations? This is where the **NGO** — Non-Governmental Organization — becomes the second wing of flight.

NGOs are not just nonprofits. When used correctly, they become **international arms of spiritual governments,** eligible for diplomatic alignment, grant funding, and recognition by global entities like the **United Nations.**

The NGO as the Global Arm of the Ministry

HEFE 360 Wealth Ministries operates with a two-body model:

508(c)(1)(A) – for domestic, faith-based, spiritually governed activity

NGO (HEFE 360 Path of Divine Wealth) – for international engagement, land acquisition, and diplomacy

Together, these two bodies allow the ministry to function like a **nation within a nation** – one rooted in spirit, protected by law, and expanding across borders.

What an NGO Unlocks

A properly structured NGO can:

- Own land, buildings, and resources in multiple countries

- Apply for **international development and spiritual education grants**

- Host programs or embassies on foreign soil

- Partner with global institutions for **health, housing, agriculture, or culture**

- Apply for **UN ECOSOC consultative status,** offering influence in international affairs

- Function as a legal **advocacy voice for the Diaspora**

The NGO is the **foreign ministry** of the 508(c) house.

UN Consultative Status: The Next Dimension

Once your NGO is formed and active, it can apply for **ECOSOC consultative status** — granting:

- The ability to speak at UN forums

- Access to UN grant opportunities

- Recognition as a **global partner for peace, justice, and development**

HEFE 360 is preparing to take this step — not for prestige, but to create spiritual infrastructure recognized by global systems.

"We do not chase the world — we position ourselves to govern within it."

How to Form the NGO

1. **Name & Purpose**

   o Choose a name that reflects your mission (e.g., Path of Divine Wealth)

   o Define global or humanitarian purpose: education, land, culture, health

2. **Legal Formation**

   o Form in a friendly country (Panama, Ghana, Kenya, U.S., etc.)

   o Create founding documents, board, mission, and registration

3. **Align with the 508**

   o Connect via doctrine, constitution, or MOU

o   Share values, leadership, and coordinated mission

4. Begin Global Programs

o   Land projects, scholarships, wellness work, Diaspora outreach

5. Apply for UN Status

o   After 1–2 years of activity, apply via the UN ECOSOC portal

o   This becomes your **spiritual foreign policy.**

Spiritual Affirmation

I build beyond borders. I minister to nations. My calling cannot be contained by state lines. Through my NGO, I rise as a servant of the world. Through divine law, I take my place at the table of nations. I am spiritual. I am sovereign. I am global. Aṣẹ

Law 17 – Ownership, Wealth & the NGO Pathway

Part 1: The Spiritual Mandate to Own

From the beginning of time, the Most High has given His people a directive: ***"Be fruitful, multiply, and have dominion."*** Dominion means ownership — not for domination, but for divine stewardship. Ownership is not greed; it is **sacred responsibility.**

In the hands of the righteous, land becomes healing. Buildings become sanctuaries. becomes a tool of liberation. But when we do not own, we **rent our identity, lease our Wealthpower, and borrow our future.**

This law is not about capitalism. It is about **returning to divine possession —** the ancestral right to hold, govern, and transfer wealth in alignment with the heavens.

Why the Ancestors Owned Land

Before the transatlantic slave trade, before colonization, before treaties were broken — we were **land holders**. We mapped star paths to farm. We protected sacred rivers. We understood that:

- To own the land is to control the food

- To control the food is to protect the body

- To protect the body is to preserve the soul

- And to preserve the soul is to walk in sovereignty

To be dispossessed was not just economic — it was **spiritual exile.** Reclaiming ownership is an act of **spiritual return.**

Wealth as a Ministry Tool

In HEFE 360 Wealth Ministries, wealth is not an idol. It is an **instrument of restoration.**

We teach:

- Land ownership through **land contracts** and ministry-led housing programs

- Revenue generation through **trust-held real estate and intellectual property**

- Intergenerational transfer through **NGO-owned holdings and grant-backed initiatives**

Wealth is not just money. Wealth is:

- Land

- Knowledge

- Bloodline

- Access

- Sovereign relationships

- Sacred contracts

We are building **new temples out of old systems**, using wealth not as chains — but as keys.

The NGO as a Global Ownership Gateway

The **NGO** becomes the legal vehicle to hold land internationally:

- Property in Africa, the Caribbean, Central America, or other Diaspora lands

- Titles held in trust or directly under NGO control

- Funded through grants, diaspora reinvestment, and ministry offerings

- Protected from seizure by foreign or domestic governments

The NGO is the **ark** — not just of mission, but of **inheritance**.

Spiritual Affirmation

I am not a renter of my destiny. I reclaim what my ancestors lost. I own what God has assigned to me. My wealth is not for vanity — it is for restoration. I build, I hold, I transfer. I plant my feet and do not move. Aṣẹ.

Part 2: Trusts, Land Contracts & Inheritance Without Interruption

To own without a **plan to pass it on is not ownership** — it is temporary possession. And in a Babylonian system built on disruption and probate, the only way to preserve wealth is to **lock it in trust.**

The trust is not a loophole. It is a **spiritual contract wrapped in legal form.** When combined with land contracts, ministry oversight, and global vehicles like NGOs, the trust becomes the **seed vault of generational wealth.**

Why Trusts Are the Backbone of Ownership

A trust is a private agreement that determines:

- **Who holds your assets**

- **Who benefits from them**

- **When and how they are transferred**

- **How they are protected from courts, taxes, and external claims**

In ministry, we use trusts not just to protect property — but to preserve **purpose**.

A sacred trust:

- Ensures the land stays in the family or community

- Assigns caretakers, not just beneficiaries

- Transfers knowledge, not just titles

- Guards the mission — not just the money

The Power of Land Contracts

In the HEFE 360 system, **land contracts** are a divine strategy to:

- Offer affordable ownership to members of the Diaspora

- Allow the ministry or NGO to act as the seller/financier

- Keep control of property until paid in full

- Avoid banks, brokers, and red tape

- Create **spiritual covenants** tied to land, not just legal ones

Example:

- Ministry owns land or housing via trust or LLC

- Buyer (seeker) enters into a 30-year land contract at 7–10% interest

- Contract includes spiritual agreements: service, rites, ancestral alignment

- Title is transferred only upon completion — but spiritual

connection is immediate

This system allows the ministry to offer **homecoming through ownership** — not just visitation.

Inheritance Without Interruption

Most wealth is lost not by theft — but by **poor planning.**

HEFE 360 teaches:

- Use **living trusts** to avoid probate

- Include **ministry or NGO as contingent beneficiaries**

- Record **video or written doctrine** with land and property to preserve values

- Ensure your NGO or trust can continue housing, feeding, and funding others beyond your lifetime

This is not about greed. It is about **spiritual continuity**. You are not just building for yourself. You are building for those yet unborn.

NGO as Global Holding Body

When an NGO owns land:

- It is **not subject to personal lawsuits**

- It can **receive international donations and grants** for development

- It can be used to provide **housing, farming, healing, or training** centers in the Diaspora

- It can establish **chapter sites** (spiritual embassies) in Africa, the Caribbean, and beyond

This is how we reclaim the land — not as individuals, but as a **spiritual nation.**

Spiritual Affirmation

I do not hold land for status. I hold it for my bloodline. I do not own to boast. I own to preserve. My trust is not just a document — it is a covenant. My contracts are sacred. My inheritance is sealed. The land remembers me — and I protect it. Aṣẹ.

Part 3: International Ownership, Ancestral Return & Diaspora Wealth Strategy

True restoration cannot happen only on U.S. soil. The roots of the Diaspora stretch back to Kemet, Ghana, Ethiopia, Nigeria, Angola, and beyond. If we only build in Babylon, we never complete the cycle. **Ancestral return** requires **international presence** — and that presence must be backed by law, land, and spiritual authority.

This is not about escape. It's about alignment. Just as Hebrew prophets, African priests, and Moorish scholars journeyed across nations to fulfill their destiny, so too must we. But this time, we move not as exiles — we move as **owners**.

Why Global Ownership Matters

To own land abroad is not just strategy — it is prophecy fulfilled:

- The **second exodus** is not just spiritual, it is physical

- The land must be prepared for return

- Communities must be built for healing, education, agriculture, and rites

- Titles must be placed in NGO or trust control to **prevent foreign exploitation**

- Youth must be trained in both local and international law to maintain continuity

When we own in **Africa, the Caribbean, and South America**, we anchor our bloodline in sacred soil again. We give our children a choice beyond Babylon.

The NGO as Your International Legal Presence

An NGO can:

- Own land in most African and Caribbean countries

- Receive **foreign donations** without U.S. tax reporting (if structured properly)

- Partner with local ministries, schools, or municipalities

- Host **healing retreats, citizenship programs, or Diaspora repatriation events**

- Lease or build homes for returning families

- Fund land acquisition through UN-aligned development grants

This is not theoretical. It is **operational sovereignty** — available now for those with vision and discipline.

Diaspora Wealth Strategy: Reversing the Flow

Most U.S. dollars flow **out of the community** through rent, taxes, and consumption. The HEFE 360 strategy reverses that flow by:

- Using U.S. income to fund land ownership abroad

- Placing property into **trusts or NGOs**, not personal names

- Renting or financing land contracts to Diaspora families

- Funding development through **grants, offerings, and book revenue**

- Leveraging international holdings to apply for **dual citizenship** and recognition

This is how you turn a **$20,000 property in Ghana** into a **$200,000 legacy anchor**. It is how you turn a humble piece of land into a living embassy of spirit.

Strategic Partnership with Ancestral Governments

Many African nations:

- Offer land incentives to Diaspora returnees

- Recognize *jus sanguinis* or spiritual repatriation

- Welcome NGOs that build clinics, schools, or farms

- Will grant residency or citizenship for land-based development

Your NGO becomes your **spiritual passport.**

Spiritual Affirmation

My wealth does not end at the ocean. My inheritance stretches across waters and time. I am not a refugee of history — I am its return. I plant in soil my ancestors once walked. I build what they were not allowed to finish. My name will be remembered on both sides of the Atlantic. Aṣẹ.

Part 5: Funding the Mission — Grants, Investors & Self-Generating Wealth

A vision without provision is delayed prophecy. The Most High does not give vision without strategy — and in this time, His people must learn to fund the mission **without begging, borrowing, or compromising.**

There is no shortage of money. There is only a shortage of **alignment**.

This part reveals how to position your ministry, trust, and NGO to **attract capital**, secure **grants and support,** and build **systems of self-generated wealth** that require no financial slavery.

You Don't Need Donations — You Need Design

Many ministries collapse financially because they rely only on offerings and emotional giving. While that is sacred, it is not **stable**.

HEFE 360 teaches that a **divine government must fund itself** through:

- Ownership of **IP and products** (books, teachings, art)

- **Land contracts** that generate long-term income

- Ministry-led **programs** (education, wellness, rites of passage)

- **Foreign and domestic grants** via NGO eligibility

Strategic **partnerships and fiscal sponsorships**

The system is not your enemy when you **outdesign it.**

The Grant Pathway for NGOs

An NGO with active programs can qualify for:

- U.S.-based private foundation grants

- International aid (education, women's health, food security, Diaspora work)

- UN-aligned development initiatives

- African/Caribbean ministry partnerships and co-investments

- Corporate philanthropic programs (Microsoft, Google, Ford Foundation, etc.)

The key is to:

- Be structured

- Be documented

- Show results (land, books, programs, people served)

- Keep your mission language clear but coded (faith-based, cultural, spiritual empowerment)

Investor Alignment – Not Just Funding, But Covenant

Sometimes the Most High sends people with money — not for their benefit, but for yours. These investors are not always banks. They may be:

- Diaspora elders looking to place funds

- Social entrepreneurs

- Faith-aligned capital groups

- Philanthropic Black wealth networks

- High-net-worth individuals seeking mission over margin

Prepare for them by:

- Keeping your structure tight (508/NGO/trust)

- Showing how **the return is spiritual, social, and generational**

- Never compromising your mission for money

- Offering private placement notes, service agreements, or land contracts as equity alternatives

You're not selling out — you're inviting others into **sacred stewardship.**

Self-Generating Wealth Systems

A self-generating ministry economy includes:

- **Intellectual property** registered to the ministry or NGO

- **Courses, certifications, and schools** under your doctrine

- **Land programs** that create monthly and equity returns

- **Digital and physical products** aligned with your teachings

- **Funding partnerships** that don't compromise your sovereignty

This is **ministry as a nation** — not just a Sunday service.

The Divine Funding Model

1. **Word** – Vision

2. **Structure** – Legal Foundation

3. Seed – Initial offerings or IP-based revenue

4. **Circulation** – Land, housing, products

5. **Expansion** – Grants, partnerships, trust strategy

6. **Preservation** – Legacy planning and trust succession

You don't chase money — you build the house, and money comes to dwell there.

Spiritual Affirmation

I do not chase wealth — I build flow. I do not beg — I position. My mission funds itself through law, trust, and alignment. Grants find me. Land yields to me. My structure attracts divine provision. I fund the vision without fear. Aṣẹ.

Law 18 – Building a Spiritual Legacy: Diaspora & Lineage

Part 1: Legacy Is Law – Bloodline, Purpose & the Eternal Return

In the way of MAAT, **nothing is separate from its source**. A seed carries the tree. A name carries the ancestors. A life carries the blueprint of those who walked before. Legacy is not history — it is **law**, encoded in blood, vibration, and responsibility.

To build a spiritual legacy is to **realign the past, present, and future** into one living continuum. It is to stand not as an individual, but as a **spiritual bridge** for your bloodline — healed, empowered, and activated.

Those of us in the Diaspora were scattered not just by ship, but by **design**. And yet, even scattered, we remain coded with the truth of who we are.

The Purpose of Remembering Your Lineage

Your lineage is your assignment. Your ancestry is your alignment.

To remember your origin is to return to:

- Your **tribal vibration**

- Your **spiritual gifts**

- Your **cultural purpose**

Your divine task in this lifetime

In Kemet and across Africa, people were not named casually. Children were named after **events, elements, and ancestral visitations.** Each name was a **vibrational spell.** Each family carried **gifts and burdens.** Reincarnation was understood — the ancestors

251

returned through blood.

When you restore your name, you restore your **purpose and protection.**

Diaspora: The Sacred Scatter

The African Diaspora did not lose its power — it was **planted** across the globe.

From the streets of Kingston to the coasts of Bahia, from the swamps of Louisiana to the deserts of Sudan — we are **fragments of one body**. And the return is not just physical — it is vibrational.

To reclaim your legacy:

- Learn your ancestral region or tribe (use DNA, oral history, intuitive guidance)

- Perform rites to honor and realign with that energy

- Name your ministry, children, and projects in sacred alignment

- Record your values, wisdom, and rituals — they are your spiritual will

- Establish a **trust or lineage temple** where your name and vibration will continue

This is not nostalgia. This is **ancestral justice.**

The Role of the Ministry in Legacy

HEFE 360 Wealth Ministries is structured not just to teach — but to **preserve**.

Our ministry:

- Holds rites of passage programs to initiate youth into sacred identity

- Documents spiritual law for descendants to live by

- Transfers land, teachings, and wealth through trusts and contracts

- Names spiritual children to carry on divine offices

- Encourages all members to trace and **reclaim their bloodline names**

This is not religion — this is **cosmic governance of the blood.**

Spiritual Affirmation

I walk with those who came before me. My name is a key. My blood is a map. I do not come from nothing — I come from power. I build not just for today, but for those I will never meet. My legacy is encoded in law, land, and light. Aṣẹ.

Part 2: Trusts, Land Contracts & Inheritance Without Interruption

In divine cultures, no child was left to define themselves by accident. From birth, they were **recognized, prepared, and initiated.** Every generation had a sacred duty to initiate the next — not just into adulthood, but into **divine identity.**

The absence of rites is what leaves modern generations wandering, seeking purpose in external validation. The presence of rites creates **anchored beings,** aligned with their purpose, ancestors, and community.

Rites of Passage in Ancestral Systems

Rites were not optional. They were:

- **Spiritual transitions** (from child to seer, from student to warrior, from healer to elder)

- **Ceremonial markers** (naming, cleansing, fasting, trials, sacred instruction)

- **Reaffirmation of bloodline power**

In Kemet, West Africa, and across the Indigenous world, rites included:

- Ritual baths and anointings

- Assigning of sacred names and totems

- Lessons in Universal Law, MAAT, and cosmology

- Public recognition of new status

- A commitment to purpose and contribution

This wasn't culture — it was **cosmic law enforcement through identity.**

Spiritual Naming and Reclaiming Identity

Your name is a **spiritual vibration.**

In the West, names were stolen, replaced, and colonized. Reclaiming your true name — whether through ancestry, spiritual revelation, or rites — is a **vibrational awakening.**

The Ministry teaches:

- Researching ancestral naming traditions (Akan, Yoruba, Kemetic, etc.)

- Listening for the soul name during meditation, dreams, or rites

- Renaming oneself as part of rebirth (aligned with Law 13: chemistry and frequency)

- Passing on names that carry **energy, meaning, and purpose**

Name your children with intention. Name your programs with frequency. Name your properties as altars. **Every name you speak is an invocation.**

Succession as a Sacred Structure

Legacy is broken when succession is left to chance. Whether by blood or by spirit, the ministry must:

- Choose successors by vibration and vision, not just title

- Prepare them through teaching, fasting, and ancestral rites

- Record succession in trust, constitution, and spiritual law

- Protect the message from dilution and distortion

You do not die with your knowledge. You **pass it encoded** into others — in ritual, in land, in instruction, in name.

This is how kingdoms rise and remain.

Spiritual Affirmation

I am not the end of my line. I am a bridge to those yet born. My name is my offering. My rites are my shield. My blood remembers. I do not die — I return in form, spirit, and legacy. Aşẹ.

Part 3: Lineage Temples, Blood Trusts & The Return of the Heir

In ancient systems, legacy wasn't an idea — it was an institution. It had structure. It had ritual. It had location. It had law. Every family was a **lineage temple,** a house of memory and destiny. When that structure was intact, wealth didn't just pass through hands — it passed through **ritualized succession.**

The modern world teaches inheritance through paperwork.

The ancestral world taught inheritance through **presence, preparation, and prophecy.**

We must now restore the **bloodline infrastructure** that ensures the preservation of land, teachings, gifts, and divine rights.

The Lineage Temple

A lineage temple is a:

- Physical or spiritual space dedicated to your family mission

- Repository of teachings, rituals, land, and laws

- Place for rites, naming, and ancestral communion

- Site for records, recordings, and the transfer of inheritance

In HEFE 360, we encourage members to:

- Choose or consecrate land (even a room or virtual archive)

- Record their spiritual teachings, vows, or affirmations to descendants

- Set up sacred calendars (birthdays, ancestral days, naming anniversaries)

- Store wills, trust documents, books, rituals, and affirmations inside this space

Make it a **center of gravity** for future heirs — not just a house, but a **home of return**

The Blood Trust

A Blood Trust is a spiritual + legal entity that holds:

- Land

- IP

- Business interests

- Ritual items

- Teachings

- Burial and rite instructions

- Succession agreements

Unlike a commercial trust, a **Blood Trust** is tied to:

- Spiritual lineage (biological or adopted)

- Rites of passage for access

- Behavior clauses (alignment with MAAT, universal law, etc.)

- Generational stewardship (each heir adds to the trust, not just receives from it)

It transforms "estate planning" into **lineage preservation.**

The Return of the Heir

An heir is not a child. An heir is a **prepared vessel.**

Every generation must:

- Identify the heir(s) through divine confirmation and teaching

- Teach them to preserve land, law, wealth, and sacred order

- Allow their energy to evolve the mission without erasing

the foundation

- Empower them to lead with **humility, justice, and ancestral awareness**

When there is no heir, the vibration dies. When the heir is prepared, the **legacy multiplies.**

This is the true resurrection: when your body is gone but your blueprint continues.

Spiritual Affirmation

I am a temple of my bloodline. I house the memory and mission of my ancestors. My trust is not just legal — it is eternal. My heir will not inherit just land — they will inherit purpose. Through order, I create continuity. Through succession, I live forever. Aṣẹ.

Law 19 – The Divine Vault: IULs, Trusts & Eternal Wealth Planning

Part 1: Wealth Without Death – The Living Legacy System

True wealth is not paper. It is **energy held in structure.** And in this age, our people must no longer rely on banks, broken systems, or a death-based economy. We must become the **banks of our own bloodlines** — living vaults of provision, protection, and permanence.

This law unveils the sacred design of:

- **IULs (Indexed Universal Life)**

- **Trusts**

- **Private lending**

- **Infinite legacy flow**

Used properly, these tools make your name into a **living economy** — one that does not die with the body.

Death-Based Wealth vs. Living Legacy

Most life insurance is built on a **death transaction:** when you die, your family gets paid.

But in the HEFE 360 system, wealth is designed to:

- Grow while you live

- Be accessed during your lifetime

- Be used to fund your mission

- Pass on **tax-free** to your heirs

259

- Be protected from lawsuits, banks, and the government

This is called the **living legacy system**, and the **IUL (Indexed Universal Life)** policy is its cornerstone.

What Is an IUL?

An **IUL** is a special type of life insurance that:

- Builds **cash value** over time (not just a death benefit)

- Earns interest based on the **stock market index,** but never loses money

- Allows you to borrow from it tax-free

- Passes wealth to heirs **tax-free and probate-free**

- Can be placed inside a **trust or ministry structure**

In short, it is a **private bank inside your family or ministry.**

Why IULs Are Spiritually Aligned

We teach IULs not just as strategy — but as **stewardship**:

- You're not waiting for tragedy — you're creating circulation

- You're not trusting banks — you're trusting divine structure

- You're not leaving your children debt — you're leaving them a **living inheritance**

- You're not buying insurance — you're **activating ancestral wealth flow**

The goal is not to die rich — it is to **live funded and die covered.**

Spiritual Affirmation

I do not wait for death to fund my family.I build now. I give now. I preserve now. My wealth grows in silence and flows by law. I am the bank. I am the vault. I am the legacy. Aṣẹ.

Part 2: Becoming Your Own Bank – Borrowing from the Vault While You Live

In the Babylonian system, you must beg banks to access the wealth you already earned. You need credit checks, approvals, and interest rates set by strangers. But in divine law, **you are the lender and the borrower,** the source and the storehouse.

With the IUL structured correctly, you become a **spiritual and financial lender to yourself** — no application needed. This is not theory. It is law-backed, tax-free, and completely under your control.

How IULs Create Private Banking Systems

An Indexed Universal Life (IUL) policy allows you to:

- Deposit funds that grow **tax-deferred**

- Access the **cash value** through policy loans — without credit checks or taxes

- Repay on your terms — or not at all

- Keep the death benefit **intact and tax-free for heirs**

You don't withdraw money — you **borrow against it**, using the policy as your own bank.

You can use it to:

- Fund real estate

- Invest in your ministry or business

- Pay for rites of passage, education, healing, or emergencies

- Re-loan it to your trust or NGO and earn from yourself

This is divine circulation. You become **the bank your ancestors never had.**

Why IUL-Based Vaults Are Superior to Traditional Banks

1. **Control**

Traditional Bank: You are just a customer using someone else's rules.

IUL Vault: You are the bank. You decide how and when to access your wealth.

2. **Access**

Traditional Bank: You must pass credit checks, applications, and approval systems.

IUL Vault: No credit check or approval needed. You access the cash value on your terms.

3. **Taxation**

Traditional Bank: You pay taxes on earned interest or withdrawn funds.

IUL Vault: You borrow against your own money — **tax-free.**

4. **Inheritance**

Traditional Bank: Bank accounts pass through probate and may be taxed or contested.

IUL Vault: Your heirs receive the **death benefit tax-free and directly,** outside probate.

5. **Privacy & Protection**

Traditional Bank: Accounts are public, traceable, and subject to garnishment.

IUL Vault: Held in trust or ministry, invisible to creditors or courts — protected wealth.

Real-World Application: HEFE 360 Model

In Own Nothing, Control Everything: The HEFE 360 Global Wealth Strategy, we teach:

"Wealth is not what you hold. Wealth is what you control from sacred distance."

The HEFE 360 model:

- Places the IUL policy inside a **trust or ministry structure**

- Has the trust **borrow against the policy** to fund land acquisition, books, or operating capital

- Ensures the **heirs inherit both the policy and the trust**

- Keeps the asset **off personal records,** protected from lawsuits or seizure

This is how wealth **moves in silence, grows without risk,** and **transfers by design.**

Spiritual Affirmation

I am not a borrower. I am the source. I lend to myself from divine order. My vault is quiet but powerful. My structure is sacred. My wealth is protected. I live funded. I die covered. I rise eternal. Aṣẹ.

Part 3: Trust-Based Design — Protecting the Vault from Babylon

Building wealth without protection is like planting crops without fencing. The wolves of Babylon — taxes, courts, debt collectors, family drama, probate — will devour your harvest unless you structure it properly. The divine solution is the trust.

A trust is not just a legal tool — it is a **spiritual shield,** a cloak of invisibility, and a code of continuity. When combined with an IUL and a 508(c)(1)(A) or NGO structure, the trust becomes the **master key of divine wealth protection.**

Why a Trust Is Non-Negotiable

When your IUL or any asset is owned in **your name**, it:

- Becomes part of your taxable estate

- Can be frozen, contested, or taxed upon death

- Can be accessed in lawsuits or child support cases

- May trigger probate and delays in access for your heirs

But when your IUL is placed in a **properly structured trust,** it:

- Skips probate entirely

- Pays out instantly, tax-free, and privately

- Protects your heirs from outsiders and court challenges

- Preserves your values by defining how funds must be used (education, rites, land, etc.)

- Can include **behavioral or spiritual clauses** (e.g., child must complete rites of passage or serve the ministry to inherit)

This is **law meeting legacy** — exactly as MAAT requires: truth, order, balance, and protection.

Ministry-Owned or Trust-Owned?

Both work — it depends on your divine assignment.

Option 1: Ministry or 508(c)(1)(A) Ownership

- Policy is owned by the ministry

- Cash value may be used to fund programs, land acquisition, or publishing

- Death benefit continues to fund the ministry's mission beyond your lifetime

Option 2: Private Trust Ownership

- Policy is owned by a family or bloodline trust

- Beneficiaries are your heirs (or their trusts)

- Gives more personal control and flexibility outside of ministry use

In the **HEFE 360 Global Wealth Strategy,** both are used:

One policy funds the mission. Another funds the family. **Both are sacred.**

Notes on Policy Structuring

- Always assign a **trust, not a person,** as the policy beneficiary

- The trust should have a **spiritual successor clause** (who leads if you transition)

- Name the ministry or NGO as a contingent beneficiary (secondary) if you want wealth to remain within the sacred structure

- Fund policies while you're young or healthy — cash value grows faster, and premiums are lower

This is how your vault becomes **untouchable** — yet eternally fruitful.

Spiritual Affirmation

I do not leave my wealth to the wind. I shield it in trust. I name its path. I control its flow.

No court decides my legacy. No bank defines my worth. What I build is protected. What I pass on is pure. My structure is sacred. My vault is invisible. Aṣẹ.

Part 4: Infinite Wealth Strategy – Seeding 3 Generations at Once

The true measure of wealth is not what you earn — it's what survives three generations. This is the ancient law of **tri-generational wealth**. In Kemet, Mali, and among sacred tribes worldwide, one generation built, the second expanded, and the third inherited with mastery.

Modern systems break this cycle through taxes, ignorance, and lack of structure. But the Divine Vault reverses that damage — and **plants one seed that feeds many roots.**

The Rule of 3: Legacy by Design

Generation 1: The Builder

- You fund the IUL and establish the trust

- You record your values, teachings, contracts, and land agreements

- You name your heirs — by blood or by spirit

Generation 2: The Steward

- Inherits access to policy loans, land, or business

- Must preserve or grow the wealth

- May add their own IUL to the trust for future heirs

Generation 3: The Multiplier

- Born into structure, not survival

- Trained from rites of passage, not trauma

- Starts life with land, funding, and purpose

This is not inheritance. This is **encoded eternity.**

Planting Multiple Vaults

In advanced structures, you:

- Fund **multiple IULs** for yourself and your heirs

- Set up a **trust-to-trust** transfer so wealth flows from one vault to another

- Establish spiritual and financial **benchmarks** (a child must complete rites, publish teachings, or serve the community to access funds)

- Assign assets like land contracts, book royalties, or business profits to flow **through the trust** into new vaults

This ensures wealth is not just **passed — it is activated.**

The Role of HEFE 360 Wealth Strategy

The book *Own Nothing, Control Everything: The HEFE 360 Global Wealth Strategy aligns with this Law by teaching:*

"Control is the inheritance. Structure is the protector. Ownership is a liability unless divinely assigned."

The HEFE 360 blueprint gives readers:

- A roadmap for "invisible wealth" through trusts and vaults

- Tools to use IULs as **economic resurrection**

- A guide to protect intellectual, spiritual, and tangible assets

- Real-life strategy to fund both ministry and family lines without ever touching Babylon

It is not just a companion — it is a **manual of spiritual currency.**

Spiritual Affirmation

I plant a seed that will never die. I fund generations I will never meet. I do not pass down pain — I pass down power. My name is written in trust. My light is stored in law. Through me, my lineage will never lack. Aṣẹ.

Law 20 – Walking in MAAT: Ancestral Tools, Rituals & Spiritual Technology

Part 1: Living the Law – Ritual as Daily Alignment

MAAT is not a concept. It is a **lifestyle, a vibration, and a discipline**. To walk in MAAT means to live in truth, reciprocity, balance, justice, and divine order — not just in words, but in **ritualized being.**

Our ancestors did not need clocks to find rhythm, nor churches to find God. They lived by the **sun, the moon, the elements, the breath, and the blood.** Ritual was not religion — it was **alignment**. It kept them in tune with the cosmos and with themselves.

Why Ritual Is Law

The body needs habits. The spirit needs rhythm. The land needs offering. The ancestors need acknowledgement.

Ritual is how we:

- Cleanse our energy

- Feed our lineage

- Call in our guidance

- Recalibrate to divine truth

- Mark sacred time and transition

In Kemetic, West African, and Indigenous practice, **ritual was the technology of alignment** — a method of clearing distortion and returning to Source.

Examples of Sacred Daily Rituals

1. Libation & Ancestral Invocation

- o   Pouring clean water with prayer at sunrise
- o   Calling ancestors by name and asking for guidance

2. Sound Healing & Frequency Work

- o   Use of tuning forks, singing bowls, drumming, or the voice
- o   Toning sacred sounds (e.g., "Ma-a-at") to clear space

3. Cleansing with Herbs & Smoke

- o   Burning sage, frankincense, palo santo, or African resins
- o   Bathing in spiritual herbs (e.g., basil, hyssop, rosemary)

4. Sacred Writing

- o   Journaling dreams, intentions, or daily reflections
- o   Keeping a "book of life" for lineage and law

5. Sun Gazing / Moon Alignment

- o   Attuning to solar energy at dawn
- o   Performing rituals on new and full moons

These are not superstition. They are **technologies of divine law,** keeping you grounded in truth while walking among chaos.

Spiritual Affirmation

I do not move blindly. I walk in rhythm. I do not forget the unseen. I honor the ancestors. Every breath is a ritual. Every act is a prayer. I align, I cleanse, I rise. MAAT is not a word — it is my way. Aṣẹ.

Part 2: Ancestral Altars, Offering Work & Elemental Law

The altar is not decoration. It is not a trend. It is a **portal** — a living interface between you and the ancestral realm. In every high culture, from Kemet to the Congo, from the Yoruba to the Taino, altars were **spiritual homes for unseen forces.**

Building and maintaining an altar is not superstition — it is **a sacred contract.** To walk in MAAT is to walk with the dead. To walk with the dead is to walk with wisdom. And to walk with wisdom is to carry **order, not chaos.**

The Purpose of the Altar

The ancestral altar is where you:

- Feed and honor your lineage

- Speak your intentions into the spirit realm

- Receive dreams, visions, and protection

- Maintain alignment and remove spiritual blockages

- Anchor your bloodline in sacred light

It is not about worship. It is about **remembrance, alignment, and guidance.**

Building an Altar Aligned with MAAT

Your altar should include:

- **A white cloth** – purity and clarity

- **Water** – memory and life-force (changed regularly)

- **A candle or flame** – divine presence and light

- **Photos or names of ancestors** – those who lived in truth

- **Offerings** – fruit, drink, food, incense, herbs, flowers

- **Spiritual tools** – shells, feathers, ankh, stones, or sacred texts

Place your altar in a quiet, respected area. Approach it with humility and purpose. Cleanse yourself before interacting. Offer with both hands.

Offering as Spiritual Reciprocity

In MAAT, giving maintains balance. Offerings are not payment — they are **vibrational exchanges.**

You offer:

- For guidance

- For clarity

- For cleansing

- In gratitude

- To feed the ones who feed you

Never beg your ancestors. Align with them. Speak clearly. Thank them. Then listen.

Elemental Law – Working with Earth, Air, Fire, Water

To be in tune with MAAT is to honor the **natural elements,** because the elements are the original deities — the first forces of law and balance.

- **Earth** – grounding, stability, land, trust, bones

- **Water** – cleansing, memory, womb, emotion

- **Fire** – transformation, passion, truth, communication

- **Air** – intellect, intuition, breath, spirit

- **Ether** – divine source, silence, the unseen

Every ritual must respect these forces. Every imbalance in life is a reflection of imbalance in the elements within and around you.

Walking in MAAT means knowing which element is active, which needs calming, and which needs calling.

Spiritual Affirmation

My altar is a gate. My offering is a key. I honor the elements — they do not forget me. The water remembers. The flame bears witness. The wind moves my prayers. The earth holds my name. I do not walk alone. I walk with order. Aşę.

Part 3: Tools of the Ancients – Astrology, Numerology & Spiritual Calculations

Long before clocks, apps, or western psychology, our ancestors mapped the soul using **astrology, numerology, and symbolic codes.** These tools were not entertainment — they were sacred sciences, woven into temples, calendars, and initiation rites.

To walk in MAAT is to understand **timing, cycles, and personal alignment.** Your birth was not random. Your name is not empty. Your numbers are not coincidence. They are all **codes of divine identity and direction.**

Astrology: The Cosmic Blueprint

Astrology, in its sacred form, reveals:

- Your **soul contract**

- Your karmic lessons

- Your strengths, triggers, timing, and spiritual destiny

- How the stars aligned when your **spirit entered the vessel**

Your **natal chart** is your spiritual GPS — a divine map left behind by your soul. No two charts are the same. In Kemetic and Dogon systems, this information determined naming, schooling, rites, and even ministry roles.

In the HEFE 360 system:

- Members are encouraged to chart their birth time and placements

- Use astrology not for ego or fear — but for **clarity and timing**

- Integrate your star code into your ministry, wealth plan, and family structure

Numerology: Vibration in Number

Numbers are more than math. They are **frequencies that govern energy.** In spiritual numerology:

- **1** is divine spark and initiation

- **2** is balance and union

- **3** is creation and voice

- **4** is foundation and stability

- **5** is freedom and transformation

- **6** is harmony and responsibility

- **7** is divinity and completion

- **8** is power and karma

- **9** is divine ending and rebirth

Your birthdate, life path, and name all carry vibrational signatures. Your phone number, address, and business names should all reflect numbers that align with your mission. MAAT is not just spiritual — it is **mathematical order.**

Sacred Timing

In ancestral systems, **nothing was done randomly.** Decisions, ceremonies, naming, and even warfare were timed according to:

- Lunar cycles

- Solar returns

- Personal year cycles

- Numerological days

- Planetary retrogrades and alignments

To walk in MAAT is to **stop forcing, rushing, or guessing,** and **instead move when the universe is open.**

Companion Journal: HEFE 360 — The Divine Map

This Law connects to the HEFE 360 astrology and numerology companion journal:

"The Divine Map: Charting Your Birthright Through Stars, Signs & Spiritual Alignment"

It will guide members to:

Track their birth chart

Record dreams and symbols

Understand numerological influences

Create personalized ritual calendars

Integrate their cosmic design with their financial and spiritual path

This is how you walk in MAAT **with data, with frequency, with law.**

Spiritual Affirmation

I do not wander — I walk in rhythm. My numbers speak. My stars remember. My body is ancient. My timing is precise. I align with the map. I honor the code. I walk in MAAT by science and soul. Aṣẹ

Part 4: Frequency, Sacred Space & Energy Hygiene

Just as the body requires bathing, the spirit requires cleansing. Just as a house must be swept, your energy field must be cleared. This is not superstition — this is **energetic maintenance,** an essential part of walking in MAAT.

You cannot hold divine law in a cluttered temple.

You cannot receive clear direction with blocked frequencies.

You cannot serve the ancestors with chaotic energy.

MAAT demands cleanliness — not just of body, but of space, sound, thought, and vibration.

The Law of Frequency

Everything vibrates. Every word, object, place, and person emits a frequency.

- High frequencies feel like peace, clarity, flow, alignment

- Low frequencies feel like confusion, fear, tension, loss

Spiritual technology is not just what you use — it's how you **tune**

- Your voice is a tuning fork

- Your thoughts are broadcasts

- Your food is frequency

- Your home is an altar

- Your relationships either amplify or drain you

To walk in MAAT is to be intentional with your frequency — always.

Sacred Space Creation

Your physical environment is a mirror of your spiritual state.

A sacred space should:

- Be clean, uncluttered, and intentional

- Contain objects of spiritual resonance (books, symbols, plants, elements)

- Have natural light, airflow, and boundaries (no confusion or chaos allowed)

- Be free of TV, gossip, and noise — protect the frequency

A sacred home is not just peaceful — it's an **extension of your temple.**

Energy Hygiene Practices

These should be done regularly — not when things go wrong, but as **preventive spiritual maintenance:**

- **Salt Baths & Foot Soaks** (with sea salt, baking soda, herbs)

- **Smoke Clearing** (sacred woods, frankincense, myrrh, copal, resins)

- **Sound Therapy** (singing bowls, tuning forks, drums, chants)

- **Daily Prayer, Breathing, & Stillness**

- **Cord Cutting** (removing unhealthy energetic ties)

- **Dream Recording** (your higher self speaks through dreams — honor them)

These tools keep your spirit sharp, your intuition clean, and your MAAT walk aligned.

Spiritual Affirmation

My body is sacred. My space is sacred. My energy is guarded. My frequency is intentional. I do not carry what is not mine. I do not dwell where chaos lives. I clean, I clear, I tune. I walk in MAAT with clarity and command. Aṣẹ.

Law 21 – Confirm the Law: Study, Question, Embody

Part 1: The Power of 21 – Completion, Mastery & the Return to Self

In sacred systems, nothing is numbered by accident. The final law of this book is not Law 21 by chance — it is by **cosmic design.**

Why 21?

- **21 = 3 x 7**

  o 3 is the number of divine creation and balance.

  o 7 is spiritual mastery and ancestral alignment.

  o Together, 21 is the law of completion — *initiation multiplied by divine order.*

- In **numerology**, 2 + 1 = 3, returning us to the principle of the sacred trinity — but now with **maturity and divine awareness.**

- In ancient traditions, 21 marks:

  o Full spiritual adulthood

  o The completion of initiation cycles

  o Divine commission into service, leadership, and stewardship

Ending your sacred constitution on Law 21 means:

The reader has graduated from follower to vessel — from seeker to source.

Part 2: Do Not Worship the Book — Confirm the Law

This book is sacred — but it is not infallible. It is a **divine offering**, not a final authority.

In the spirit of MAAT:

- You are required to **research what you've read**

- You are encouraged to **question, meditate, and seek your own confirmations**

- You are commanded to **embody truth — not blindly follow it**

Spiritual sovereignty is not obedience — it is **alignment through understanding.**

"Do not just quote the law. Become it."

Part 3: You Now Hold the Power to Build Your Own

You now have the knowledge to:

- Form your own **508(c)(1)(A) faith-based ministry**

- Establish an **NGO as your international arm**

- Create your own **trusts, land programs, rites of passage**, and wealth systems

- Publish your own sacred text, constitution, or doctrine

- Lead your family and lineage with clarity, protection, and structure

Nothing in this book was given to keep you dependent — it was given to awaken the **divine architect within you.**

If you choose to serve under HEFE 360, you are welcome.

If you choose to build your own, you are still in alignment.

We are not here to create followers.

We are here to create **sovereign builders of divine order.**

Spiritual Affirmation – The Closing Seal

I have received the law. I have remembered who I am. I study. I question. I confirm. I do not worship the structure — I become the living temple. I will build with truth. I will serve with balance. I am no longer a seeker — I am the law in motion. Aṣẹ.

REFERENCE & INSPIRATION PAGE

Sacred Sources, Ancestral Wisdom & Foundational Texts

This sacred book, **HEFE 360: Universal Law and Divine Order,** was not created from personal intellect alone. It is the result of ancestral remembrance, spiritual downloads, lived experience, and divine alignment with sacred systems across time.

We honor and acknowledge the following sources as spiritual inspiration and structural alignment:

Ancestral & Cosmological Foundations

- **The 42 Laws of MAAT** (Kemet, Ancient Egypt)

- **The Book of Coming Forth by Day** (commonly referred to as The Egyptian Book of the Dead)

- **Dogon Cosmology** (Mali, West Africa)

- **Yoruba Ifá System** and the sacred Odu corpus

- **Moorish, Ethiopian, and Nubian dynastic law systems**

- **The Divine Feminine Traditions** of Black and Indigenous women across the Diaspora

Sacred Strategy & Financial Structure

Own Nothing, Control Everything: The HEFE 360 Global Wealth Strategy

- o Authored by HEFE 360 Global Inc.

- o A spiritual and strategic manual for trust-based wealth, ministry protection, and global positioning

HEFE 360: The Divine Map (Astrological and Numerological Journal)

- o A spiritual navigation journal companion for decoding your birthright, numbers, and alignment

The Vienna Convention on Diplomatic Relations (1961)

- o Cited for its legal definition of diplomatic immunity and the framework for global recognition of sovereign spiritual missions

Modern Influences (Law, Finance & Movement)

- Trust Law & Estate Structuring from legacy Black wealth practitioners

- Indexed Universal Life (IUL) frameworks used by Infinite Banking advocates

- NGO templates from United Nations ECOSOC recognition standards

- Diaspora land repatriation models in Ghana, South Africa, and the Caribbean

Living Teachers, Elders & Spiritual Channels

We honor the unnamed elders, ancestors, spiritual mothers, and initiates whose prayers, labor, and bloodline wisdom form the root of this work. To all the forgotten names whose teachings survived by vibration — **we see you, we name you, we build in your memory**. Aṣẹ.

GLOSSARY OF TERMS

Definitions for Spiritual Alignment & Legal Understanding

508(c)(1)(A)

A section of the U.S. Internal Revenue Code that allows faith-based organizations to be automatically tax-exempt and sovereign from state interference. Not required to file or apply for status. Covered by the First Amendment.

Ancestral Altar

A sacred space where offerings, prayers, and invocations are made to one's ancestors. Used for guidance, remembrance, protection, and spiritual alignment.

Aṣẹ (ah-SHAY)

A West African spiritual affirmation meaning "so let it be" or "the power to make things happen." Often used to seal declarations of truth.

Blood Trust

A spiritually governed legal trust created to preserve wealth, land, and teachings for one's bloodline or spiritual heirs. Includes ancestral and behavioral requirements.

Diaspora

Refers to the global dispersal of African peoples due to colonization, slavery, and migration. Also seen as sacred planting — the scattering of divine DNA across the earth.

Divine Order

Universal structure governed by truth, balance, and spiritual law. Refers to MAAT and the natural, sacred systems encoded in all of creation.

HEFE 360

A sacred framework of law, wealth, alignment, and ancestral return. The ministry name stands for Holistic Economic Freedom & Empowerment — 360 degrees of divine order and wealth.

Indexed Universal Life (IUL)

A tax-advantaged life insurance policy that grows in cash value based on stock market performance. Used in HEFE 360 as a wealth-building tool and private banking system.

Infinite Banking

A strategy that allows one to borrow from the cash value of their own IUL policy, becoming their own source of funding. Protected and tax-free when structured correctly.

Law of MAAT

Ancient Kemetic principle of universal balance. Includes truth, justice, reciprocity, harmony, order, and righteousness. The spiritual foundation of this ministry.

Legacy Temple / Lineage Temple

A physical or spiritual place designated to preserve family teachings, rituals, wealth, land, and legal structures. Center for rites of passage and ancestral remembrance.

Ministry-Owned LLC

A limited liability company owned by a 508(c)(1)(A) ministry, used to generate revenue while maintaining tax-exempt status. Must serve the spiritual mission.

NGO (Non-Governmental Organization)

An independent international organization created for

humanitarian or spiritual work. Used as the global arm of the HEFE 360 ministry.

Numerology

The sacred science of number vibration. Used to interpret destiny, names, dates, and life paths through numbers.

Rites of Passage

Spiritual and ceremonial transitions from one life stage to another (e.g., childhood to adulthood, student to leader). Used to initiate heirs and prepare successors.

Spiritual Technology

Ancestral tools and rituals — including sound, astrology, herbs, breathwork, and offerings — used to maintain energetic alignment and spiritual clarity.

Trust (Legal)

A legal entity used to hold and manage assets on behalf of beneficiaries. In HEFE 360, trusts are sacred structures used to protect divine wealth and family lineage.

MINISTRY CONTACT & COMMISSIONING PAGE

This is your divine seal — the bridge between the Word and the Work.

Produced & Published By:

HEFE 360 WEALTH MINISTRIES

A 508(c)(1)(A) Faith-Based Ministry

Operating in Divine Order under First Amendment protection

Structured for global service, ancestral legacy, and spiritual governance

Global Outreach Arm:

HEFE 360 Path of Divine Wealth (NGO)

Serving the Diaspora, land repatriation programs, spiritual rites, and humanitarian missions

Official Works Referenced in This Doctrine:

Own Nothing, Control Everything: The HEFE 360 Global Wealth Strategy

HEFE 360: The Divine Map (Astrological & Numerological Companion Journal)

Contact Information:

Website: www.hefe360wealthministry.org

Email: info@hefe360wealthministry.org

Global Reach: U.S. | Africa | The Caribbean | Latin America | Diaspora Worldwide

Spiritual Use & Reproduction:

This book is not for commercial replication without spiritual authorization.

It is a **living document** of HEFE 360 law, protected under divine and constitutional right.

It may be quoted, taught, or referenced only in **alignment with MAAT** — truth, reciprocity, order, and justice.

Final Declaration:

You now hold the code. The next move is yours.

May you build your own ministry, activate your lineage, protect your wealth, and govern your destiny in alignment with sacred law. The ancestors are watching. Your future is waiting. The scroll is now in your hands. Aṣẹ.

HEFE360
WEALTH MINISTRIES

www.ingramcontent.com/pod-product-compliance
Lightning Source LLC
Chambersburg PA
CBHW021219130626
46554CB00004B/1287